LANGUAGE AND

Dorothy
Celia Genishi

ADVISORY BOARD: *Richard Allington, Kathryn Au, Bernice Cullinan, Colette Daiute, Anne Haas Dyson, Carole Edelsky, Mary Juzwik, Susan Lytle, Django Paris, Timothy Shanahan*

continued

For volumes in the NCRLL Collection (edited by JoBeth Allen and Donna E. Alvermann) and the Practitioners Bookshelf Series (edited by Celia Genishi and Donna E. Alvermann), as well as other titles in this series, please visit www.tcpress.com.

Language and Literacy Series, *continued*

Letting Go
of
Literary Whiteness

Antiracist Literature Instruction for White Students

Carlin Borsheim-Black
Sophia Tatiana Sarigianides

Foreword by Timothy J. Lensmire

TEACHERS COLLEGE PRESS

TEACHERS COLLEGE | COLUMBIA UNIVERSITY

NEW YORK AND LONDON

Published by Teachers College Press, 1234 Amsterdam Avenue, New York, NY 10027

Copyright © 2019 by Teachers College, Columbia University

Figure 2.1 created by Victor Juhasz for *Rolling Stone*. Used with permission of the creator.

Library of Congress Cataloging-in-Publication Data is available at loc.gov

Library of Congress Control Number: 2019947276

ISBN 978-0-8077-6305-6 (paper)
ISBN 978-0-8077-6306-3 (hardcover)
ISBN 978-0-8077-7762-6 (ebook)

Printed on acid-free paper

Manufactured in the United States of America

For our children:
Marcus, Miles, and Mia,
Alexandros and Phaedon

Contents

Foreword

There's magic in Carlin Borsheim-Black and Sophia Sarigianides' book, and I've been trying to figure out how that magic works.

It reminds me of what happens when, in my work with White future teachers, we read and discuss George Lipsitz's (1995) historical analysis of how progressive, social democratic policies in the United States since the 1930s have, nevertheless, benefitted White people far more than people of color. When these students read, for example, that during the New Deal the "Social Security Act excluded farm workers and domestics from coverage, effectively denying those disproportionately minority sectors of the work force protections and benefits routinely channeled to Whites" (p. 372), there's a kind of relaxation or exhalation of stress and guilt, because Lipsitz is saying that they are not responsible for legislation that was signed into law by President Roosevelt in 1935.

However, soon enough, Lipsitz has demanded that his White readers take up a different responsibility than that we feel guilty for the actions and violences of White people in the past. He demands that we face the present "openly and honestly"—which, as Lipsitz argues so persuasively, we can only do as White people when we acknowledge our society's past and continuing "possessive investment in Whiteness" (p. 384).

I do not claim some magical transformation of White future teachers' thinking and feeling because of Lipsitz's writing and my use of it. That said, something important often happens, and I think it is because of how Lipsitz's text shifts our responsibilities, as White people, from unhelpful things (like feeling guilty) to potentially helpful things, like understanding and acting against how White supremacy is reproduced in our society.

Sophia and Carlin's book is startling in how openly and honestly it takes up the problem of how to teach about racism, using literature, in White schools. As I read, I kept marveling at how courageous and direct and clear their writing is. If Lipsitz's history lesson lessens the guilt of White readers so they can confront the workings of our White supremacist society, then Carlin and Sophia's writing seeks to neutralize the fear and anxiety that many White teachers experience when they imagine teaching about racism with White students.

The authors combat this fear and anxiety in a number of ways. They identify and address aspects of this fear explicitly, including worries about losing both rapport with students and control of classroom discussions. For those who worry that such teaching takes away from the study of literature, there are brilliant, chapter-length demonstrations—with Kwame Alexander's *The Crossover,* Mark Twain's *Huck Finn,* and Harper Lee's *To Kill a Mockingbird*—of how the study of race, Whiteness, and racism actually opens up possibilities for meaningful and critical work with literature by students. And at every moment, Sophia and Carlin remind their readers that the authors of this book have also been fearful, have not known enough, have made mistakes that haunt them—and that all they could do was keep studying and learning and trying.

One of the best tricks of this book, however, is that it shows teachers that they can draw on everyday skills and practices—ones that are already part of their work—to teach about racism through literature. Too often, addressing racism in English classrooms has meant something more like not addressing it—vague goals of "exposure" and hoping to "discuss it when it comes up" have usually carried the day. In contrast, Carlin and Sophia make the straightforward argument that if we want to teach about racism, then we should teach about racism. English teachers have objectives for their teaching—so articulate objectives that zero in on specific race concepts and that tie these concepts to literature learning. Teachers use these objectives to plan instruction and assess learning—so do that. There's a matter-of-factness to all of this that will, I think, inspire courage. (What I can't quite figure out is how Sophia and Carlin pull off this matter-of-factness while also explaining complex racial theory and sharing sophisticated readings of literature. There's some very good writing here.)

In other words, the magic of Carlin and Sophia's book is that it makes clear that there is no magic required for teaching about racism with literature in White schools. What's required is a desire for something better and a lot of hard, smart work.

—*Timothy J. Lensmire*

REFERENCE

Lipsitz, G. (1995). The possessive investment in whiteness: Racialized social democracy and the "White" problem in American studies. *American Quarterly, 47*(3), 369–387.

Acknowledgments

I (Carlin) knew for a long time that there should be "a book" focused on teaching about racism through literature study with White students, and I had ideas to contribute to that book, but the project itself felt too big to do alone. When Sophia and I started teaching and reading together, I thought, *this* is how a book might get done. I am so grateful to Sophia for agreeing to partner on this project. She is a relentless force for doing antiracist work, and through our partnership I have grown so much more than I could have on my own.

Five years ago, I (Sophia) sloppily attempted to do antiracist work with my teacher candidates, feeling completely inept. So I made an academic wish: *Please*, someone apprentice me to learn how to do this without making me feel awful about what I don't know. Then Carlin's 2015 article came out. At least I can do *this*, I thought. I invited Carlin to Skype into my methods course that fall, which launched our first conversation. So in 2016, barely knowing each other, we decided to start reading together and meeting online to dialogue. This relationship, the ideas that flourished as a result, the courage I felt working next to someone on this project, changed everything about my teaching around race. I will forever be grateful to Carlin for this.

We have many others to thank as well. We are so lucky to have had such important mentors for this journey. Tim Lensmire cheered us on, connected us with critical colleagues, and offered a model for thoughtful scholarship through his work in critical Whiteness studies. Dorinda Carter Andrews first introduced Carlin to critical race theory (CRT) in a graduate seminar at Michigan State University, and Carlin continues to draw on her readings and feedback.

Critical friends have continued to push our own journey toward racial consciousness. We thank: Nicola Martin, for responding to phone calls about parenting a Black son as a White mom; Shirley Wong and Carol Bailey for modeling what institutional work on racism looks like; Kristin McIllhagga, whose ongoing commitment to antiracist work continues to serve as a model and a guide; Matt Knieling, whose collaboration on an early research project informed Carlin's thinking. And also the many colleagues of color in our field whose Facebook posts we follow carefully, learning from a distance the so-much that we cannot understand as White women doing this work.

Many colleagues have generously offered feedback on drafts: Tim Lensmire, Nicola Martin, Mary Juzwik, Justin Grinage, Sarah Rohlfs, and Naoko Akai-Dennis, We appreciate you. Also, several cohorts of Sophia's students validated ideas in the chapters. The book would not be what it is without you.

To the librarians who tracked down copies of materials—and helped with referencing—Suz Tirrano and Becca Brody, thank you. To Emily Todd and Vanessa Diana, thank you for leading us to Chestnutt, and critical views of *Huckleberry Finn*, and to Regina Smialek, thank you for your help always!

Many thanks to Olga Hubard, the brilliant and generous artist whose work is featured in the cover design.

To our students: it is *for* you and *because of* you that we pushed forward with this project, especially when we doubted ourselves. For your trust in us as we fumbled through strategies, and prodded you with difficult questions, you inspire us. Special thanks to Carlin and Sophia's Fall 2016 methods students; Sophia's Spring 2018 graduate students; to Emily Cook, who agreed to study these questions for an entire year while teaching; and Andrew Mertes, Christine Luongo, Julianna Campbell, and Jen Cupp. The world of a teacher changes with students like all of you.

To our families, who put up with our school pick-up and drop-off cell conversations, urgent requests for coverage to settle an issue in a chapter, for watching films on race with us on date nights—you made sure we had the space to create this book, and we love you. James, Stuart, Alexandros, Marcus, Phaedon, Miles, and baby Mia: This book is for all of you, and for us.

CHAPTER 1

Teaching About Racism Through Literature in White Schools

> The Dreamers will have to learn to struggle themselves, to understand that the field for the Dream, the stage where they have painted themselves white, is the deathbed of us all.
>
> —Ta-Nehisi Coates, *Between the World and Me*

Right from the start, we want to acknowledge that what has driven our work on teaching about race and racism via literary study has been our longstanding awareness that, as White English teachers, we were not doing a good enough job addressing race and racism with our own students.

This is a difficult admission. We are both teacher educators, earning our livelihood preparing English teachers. Our jobs, and the success of the teachers whom we instruct, depend, at least in part, on our expertise in a range of methods and theories surrounding the teaching of English. Long before we began teaching and studying English education, we both were very committed to social equity issues, especially those focused on race. And yet, for a long time, we struggled to address race and racism effectively in our own classrooms.

One of the main problems tied to race and English teaching centers on a majority-White teaching force working in majority-minority schools. As a result, the field has paid a lot of attention to shifting the perspectives of White teachers to work equitably with youth of color, an effort that includes preparing teachers to employ culturally sustaining pedagogies (e.g., Paris & Alim, 2017). Eager to engage with racially equitable teaching practices, we, too, embraced the strategies of incorporating texts written by and about people of color; of ensuring that we engaged with all students and their families and communities by thinking about the "funds of knowledge" they brought to the English classroom (Moll, Amanti, Neff, & Gonzalez, 1992); and of affirming the diverse ways students engage in speaking and writing, especially when it diverges from Standardized English (Baker-Bell, 2017; Greenfield, 2011). Because youth of color continue to be underserved by our nation's schools, these methods for engaging with youth of color in

1

ways that are equitable, affirming, and rigorous are absolutely necessary (Morrell, 2015).

Yet, this framing of the problem of racism in English classrooms did not reflect the challenges we experienced in our own classrooms. For example, Carlin spent several years teaching in rural and small-town communities that were predominantly White. In those contexts, her challenge was to help White students see and acknowledge racism in literature, in society today, and in themselves, usually in the context of a curriculum that also centered Whiteness. Similarly, when we began our careers as English educators in White-dominant universities preparing teachers who came from primarily White schools, some of whom expressed plans to return to teach in or near their rural and racially homogeneous small towns, culturally sustaining strategies did not match the problems we were encountering. And while scholarship in the field described the challenges we were experiencing and encouraged us to carry on with the work of teaching about racism with White students, we found few resources that helped us envision what that work might look like in classrooms.

For these and many other reasons, when we both first attempted to address race and racism in the classroom, we struggled. We were not accustomed to discussing Whiteness in our teaching. We resisted "pushing too hard" on students who voiced problematic racial ideologies like colorblindness. We were worried about the unpredictability and likely volatility of conversations about racism. Although we taught literature that featured racism and addressed race in whole-group discussions, classroom talk often ended up recycling shallow understandings of racism. More recently, as we have encouraged new teachers to head into schools and address racism directly, we have seen ourselves in those new teachers' struggles to translate their commitment and evolving understandings about racism into practice.

We want to share some of the questions that drove us to focus on the problem of addressing race and racism in predominantly White English classrooms. Some of these questions are our own; others have been voiced by teachers in the field. We wonder whether some of you have worried about similar questions:

- Is racism an appropriate subject for English classrooms?
- Isn't it enough that I teach texts by and about people of color?
- Isn't it enough that I care about and respect all my students, especially students of color?
- If we focus on racism, will it take away from other important goals for literature instruction?
- Do I know enough about race and racism, especially as a White teacher, to guide student learning?
- What is there to say about racism in literature besides how awful it is?

- What if students, parents, or administrators disagree with a focus on racism in literary study? How do I make the case for this focus?

To negotiate these questions and others like them, this book proposes *antiracist literature instruction* as a framework English teachers can use to carry out literature-based units that make teaching about race and racism a deliberate and systematic part of the curriculum in White-dominant schools. In the next sections, we guide you through the research and scholarship we draw from to shape this approach, starting with our focus on White contexts.

WHY FOCUS ON WHITE EDUCATIONAL CONTEXTS?

Does a focus on White contexts center Whiteness and continue to privilege White students? Our response is that we understand White supremacy in the United States to be a White problem. The questions listed above emerge almost entirely as a result of White privilege, of White segregation that isolates White people from people of color in schools and communities, which makes the discussion of race and racism *seem* as though it is a matter for people of color only. It is not. As White teachers, we must shoulder responsibility for interrupting racism in our classrooms, without always relying on our colleagues of color to take the lead in this work (Tanner, 2019). In our teaching in White-dominant contexts, when White students share that they have not considered their Whiteness before, we must recognize that this omission, this silencing in their lives and in our own, must be rectified. We must understand that it is our role as White educators to do this work and that this work is not optional.

The framing quotation of this chapter is taken from the last pages of Ta-Nehisi Coates's *Between the World and Me* (2015), an extended open letter to his teenage son on the evening of yet another exculpation of a White police officer who had killed Michael Brown, a Black youth. In writing this epistolary book, Coates follows in the tradition of James Baldwin's open letter to his nephew on the 100th anniversary of the Emancipation Proclamation, "My Dungeon Shook," published in the opening pages of *The Fire Next Time* (1963). In both texts, the authors attempt to offer consolation, explanation, and resolve as Black men speaking to Black male family members about the irrefutable fact that history and the present moment demonstrate that White people are not *mature* enough (Baldwin) or do not *care* enough (Coates) about Black people to stop racism. They wrote these letters more than 50 years apart and yet their messages echo each other with the same insistence on Whites' refusal to do the work necessary to *begin* to reverse the tide of racism for the sake of all Americans.

In writing our book, we know we are the Dreamers that Coates references in our opening epigraph. We wrote this book to begin the process of re-painting the stage where we have painted ourselves White, to expose the institutional, societal, epistemological, and interpersonal racism that undergirds our Whiteness, our White privilege. We also see very clearly that our work as English teachers, if continued without thinking and acting from an antiracist perspective, perpetuates racism through the texts in our book rooms and the ways we teach them. Our English classrooms, in White-dominant contexts, are the *perfect* place for taking on Coates's challenge to do this antiracist work. Our book aims to show you how to join us and others in our field in this urgent political project.

In our experiences teaching in White-dominant schools, we began to realize that while culturally sustaining pedagogy (e.g., Paris & Alim, 2017) aims at curriculum and instruction that are *affirming* for students of color, what we needed was an approach that aimed at *disrupting* traditional curriculum and instruction for White students. Teaching White students about race, racism, and Whiteness requires direct instruction, scaffolding, and continued support in order to teach students to acknowledge their own racial identity, to name ways that racism works, and to apply new understandings to the world around them (Kailin, 2002).

Research, as well as our own experiences, illuminates the particular challenges of teaching about racism with White students. White students tend to resist—sometimes subtly and sometimes less subtly—instruction that asks them to question taken-for-granted assumptions tied to race (e.g., Asher, 2007; Gordon, 2005; Marx & Pennington, 2003; Sleeter, 2011). English teachers and students often engage in White talk, a term used to describe subtle strategies White people use to skirt discussions about racism (Haviland, 2008; Lewis, Ketter, & Fabos, 2001; McIntyre, 1997). Discussions of racism can become emotional and unpredictable when students do engage (Amobi, 2007). In fact, Sassi and Thomas (2008) describe a "powder keg" exploding in their classroom when several White male students made the argument that slavery actually benefited African Americans.

This research has helped to validate our experiences in our own classrooms by describing the ways antiracist teaching sometimes breaks down. At the same time, we do not wish to contribute to deficit views of White students' reactions to antiracist teaching. Our goal is to understand the complexities of students' responses, responses that make perfect sense given that the emphasis within this antiracist work is on *disrupting* racial ideologies that have been reinforced in White contexts. As a student in Sophia's course on antiracism in literature teaching said in class discussion, "I've never heard of Whiteness described so negatively before."

While we aim to be thoughtful about what antiracist teaching asks of White students, we are also cognizant of the fact that framing the teaching of racism for White students may risk silencing or marginalizing the experiences and needs of a small number of students of color in White-dominant classrooms. Developing antiracist strategies for working with White students without ignoring the needs of students of color matters greatly. This book offers strategies for attending to this challenge in English classrooms.

Finally, when we use the phrase "White-dominant," we mean educational contexts in which currently—or in the recent past—student demographics and communities are predominantly White. Research has shown that even in contexts that currently reflect a racially diverse student body, but where that racial diversity resulted from a recent shift in demographics, Whiteness may continue to dominate ideologically (e.g., Beach, Thein, & Parks, 2008). Often, White-dominant contexts also are characterized by curriculum that overrepresents White perspectives and instruction that privileges White ways of knowing and being in the classroom to the detriment of students of color. In White-dominant contexts such as these, students of color, too, can internalize racist ideologies (Huber, Johnson, & Kohli, 2006; Lipsky, 1987). As English teachers, we must be aware of the role we play in maintaining the racial status quo of White supremacy in the ways we engage all students via literary study.

Before moving on, we want to acknowledge that the position that we are advocating for English teachers is a vulnerable one. As university educators promoting these strategies, we have some protection because we are teaching future teachers, not secondary students. We have a professional impetus to do this work with the backing of standards for the preparation of English teachers. In 2012, the National Council of Teachers of English (NCTE) shaped guidelines that require new teachers to demonstrate preparation around specific social justice goals: "Candidates plan and implement English language arts and literacy instruction that promotes social justice and critical engagement with complex issues related to maintaining a diverse, inclusive, equitable society" (NCTE, 2012). Although there are many ways for teachers to demonstrate this skill, engaging in antiracist literary study is one significant way to do so.

But, positioning middle and high school English teachers to engage their students in explorations of Whiteness and racism can be risky. We take this seriously. Teachers we know have faced professional consequences for taking on this work without adequate local support within their school community—and, at the time, without the help of adequate discipline-based practices. We agree with Berchini (2019) that the *contexts* in which teachers take on antiracist goals matter and that any perceived "failures" in reaching these goals are absolutely not dependent solely on individual teachers being "not committed enough" to social justice goals. Regardless, teachers will need discipline-specific strategies to see what this could look like.

That said, secondary English teachers may feel bolstered by support for antiracist work from the field of English education. NCTE signals the need for such an emphasis in their position regarding race and English teaching in the Statement Affirming #BlackLivesMatter. In it, NCTE (2015b) urges "English educators to use classrooms to help as opposed to harm, to transform our world and raise awareness of the crisis of racial injustice." While they cite antiracist education for providing equitable education for Black and Brown students, they also "seek a parallel revolution in curricula, instructional models and practices, assessment approaches, and other facets of education that would lead to a future free from the barriers of prejudice, stereotyping, discrimination, and bias." We see our work in this book as a response to this call.

WHY TEACH ABOUT RACISM VIA LITERARY STUDY?

Our understandings of race and racism are informed by critical race theory. CRT developed out of the civil rights movement and critical legal studies as a way to name and explain how racism works systemically. CRT is based on a few foundational tenets (Delgado & Stefancic, 2001; Ladson-Billings & Tate, 1995). In this section, we connect understandings of racism stemming from CRT to literature curriculum and instruction with implications for antiracist education.

CRT Assumes That Racism Is Endemic

Incidents of racism are neither coincidental nor isolated; racism is pervasive in American society because it is woven into the fabric of laws, policies, systems, and institutions from the Constitution to citizenship to the legal system to the educational system to language to land ownership to the accumulation of intergenerational wealth. As a result, racism applies not only to individual beliefs, prejudices, and behaviors, but also to the ways in which it operates systematically and materially to privilege some and marginalize others.

Within the realm of English education, racism is woven into the fabric of traditional language, literacy, and literature curriculum, through the overvaluing of Eurocentric grammar rules at the expense of African American language (Baker-Bell, 2017; Smitherman, 1999) and the prioritization of White authors over literature representing experiences of people of color (e.g., Butler, 2017; Johnson, Jackson, Stovall, & Baszile, 2017; Kirkland, 2013), to name just two examples.

Within literary studies more specifically, Morrison (1992) calls attention to ways that racism is woven into the fabric of literature. Morrison explains that American literature is characterized by underlying and often invisible racial ideologies that have played a central role in constructing Whiteness in the United States. Whiteness, Morrison argues, has been defined in American literature largely in terms of what it is not—Black:

> Just as the formation of the nation necessitated coded language and purposeful restriction to deal with the racial disingenuousness and moral frailty at its heart, so too did the literature, whose founding characteristics extend into the twentieth century, reproduce the necessity for codes and restriction. Through significant and underscored omissions, startling contradictions, heavily nuanced conflicts, through the way writers peopled their work with signs and bodies of this presence—one can see that a real or fabricated Africanist presence was crucial to their sense of Americanness. (p. 6)

In other words, literature does not simply *reflect* race and racism in American society; literature has played a role in *constructing* race and racism in American society. Atticus Finch could not be Atticus Finch without Tom Robinson. Huck Finn could not be Huck Finn without Jim. Even when plots and themes do not make racism central, Morrison argues, there is often an underlying "Africanist" presence. Tom Buchanan's power and status are contrasted with his concern about "the rise of the colored empire." George and Lennie are characterized in contrast to Crooks.

While Morrison's argument references mostly canonical and American literature, CRT makes it clear that all literature curriculum is racialized; all literature curriculum teaches lessons about race and racism. In other words, teaching about race or racism through literature study is not optional; there is no way to remain neutral. Antiracist education involves deliberately challenging racist structures in and through our curriculum and instruction (Kailin, 2002).

CRT Challenges Colorblindness and Abstract Liberalism

CRT challenges dominant racial ideologies, like colorblindness and abstract liberalism, which obfuscate the realities of racism under a discourse of equality or equal opportunity. For example, the term *abstract liberalism* describes a worldview based on notions of equal opportunity, meritocracy, and individual effort. Bonilla-Silva (2013) explains that "by framing race-related issues in the language of liberalism, Whites can appear 'reasonable' and even 'moral' while opposing almost all practical approaches to deal with *de facto* racial inequality. For instance, by using the tenets of the free market ideology in the abstract, they can oppose affirmative action as a violation of the norm of equal opportunity" (p. 28). He offers an example to illustrate. A female college student says:

> I don't think they [people of color] should be provided with unique opportunities. I think that they should have the same opportunities as everyone else . . . I don't think that just because they're a minority that they should, you know, not meet the requirements, you know. (p. 31)

On the surface, this young woman seems to be arguing for equality based on the idea that everyone should have equal opportunities. However, her rationale ignores effects of past and present racism on the social, economic, and educational status of people of color. By saying "they should have the same opportunities as everyone else," this student is, essentially, defending racial inequality. This worldview is based on assumptions that the world is a meritocracy where anyone who works hard will succeed.

Abstract liberalism is closely tied to colorblindness, another kind of racist ideology, which often is reflected in comments such as, "I don't see color; I see people. People are all the same." Those who operate with a colorblind worldview argue that acknowledging racism makes the problem worse. Although colorblindness seems to operate on a desire to overcome racism, it is, itself, an insidious form of racism. Colorblindness not only denies people of color a part of their identity connected with their racial, cultural, and linguistic heritage; it invalidates individuals' experiences with racism and oppression. It shuts down important conversations that are necessary to interrupting racism.

Literature is often complicit in constructing and reinforcing ideologies that disguise, deny, minimize, and justify racism. For example, what role has a novel like *To Kill a Mockingbird* played in shaping popular thinking about the history and present-day legacies of racism? *To Kill a Mockingbird* has been one of the top two most frequently taught texts in the United States for many years (Applebee, 1993; Stallworth, Gibbons, & Fauber, 2006), one of the most widely read novels in the country in and out of schools, and often one of *the* definitive texts through which students read about racism in the United States. Why *this* story? Such questions have led to debates across the United States about whether to continue teaching the novel. It is a rich and complex story of great appeal and literary complexity, to be sure, but there are many, many rich and complex novels to be read and taught. Perhaps *To Kill a Mockingbird* is so popular precisely because it tells a story about racism that fits within, rather than challenges, dominant racial ideologies. (We present a full CRT analysis of the novel in Chapter 5.) How should English teachers respond? Should we stop teaching *To Kill a Mockingbird*?

Antiracist education can equip students with tools for critically analyzing examples of racism and racist ideologies (Kailin, 2002). DiAngelo (2016) asserts, "Most white people have never been given direct or complex information about racism before, and often cannot consciously recognize, understand, or articulate much about it" (p. 16). Antiracist education focuses on rectifying these gaps and silences in White students' educational experiences by providing students with understandings of the larger societal and historical contexts of racism.

CRT Values the Voices and Experiences of People of Color

CRT argues that by virtue of their experiences with racism, people of color are in a position to speak with authority about the nature of race and racism in a way that White people are not. CRT places value on the personal experiences and stories of people of color as a means of building solidarity, inspiring change, and challenging dominant ideology. CRT emphasizes the need for counterstories, which "aim to cast doubt on the validity of accepted premises or myths, especially ones held by the majority" (Delgado & Stefancic, 2001, p. 144). Counterstories are not counterstories simply because they are told by people of color; they are counterstories because they challenge dominant narratives about things like the American dream or meritocracy.

This tenet is fundamentally important for thinking about our literature selections. Research indicates that literature curriculum continues to favor works written by White authors, particularly White men (Applebee, 1993; Stallworth et al., 2006). The Whiteness of traditional curriculum teaches both students of color and White students racialized lessons about whose stories matter, whose voices are prioritized, and whose version of history is acknowledged (e.g., Haddix & Price-Dennis, 2013). And this issue goes beyond simply including texts by and about African Americans. For example, Butler's (2017) work emphasizes injustices related to the omission of Black women's voices in particular, noting how infrequently students encounter Black women's autobiographies and memoirs—especially about Black female revolutionaries—in typical literature curriculum.

Antiracist education encourages teachers to challenge curriculum that overrepresents dominant racial perspectives with alternative points of view designed to more accurately and fully represent history and society.

CRT Prioritizes Social Action

CRT scholars urge educators, policymakers, community activists, and others to move past theoretical discussions to make a difference in their communities and fields. Antiracist education, too, depends on taking action. It is not enough to be nonracist or even passively antiracist; antiracist educators must do something to transform unequal power relations in practice (DiAngelo, 2016).

We, like other English educators (e.g., Baker-Bell, Butler, & Johnson, 2017; Johnson et al., 2017; Morrell, 2005), view English language arts as an important site for working toward racial justice. And, of course, literature instruction in particular can be a powerful tool for social change.

Like others in our field, we have found racial literacy to be useful for getting more specific about what taking action can look like in terms of student learning (e.g., Bolgatz, 2005; Rogers & Mosley, 2006; Sealey-Ruiz & Greene, 2015). Twine (2004) initially described racial literacy as social practices that "race cognizant" White parents engaged in to help their adopted children of color deal with and resist racism in the interest of transforming racial hierarchies (p. 881). These social practices included things like discussing and evaluating representations of people of color in media and texts and developing vocabulary for describing experiences with race outside the home in racialized terms. Building on this early work, DiAngelo (2016) offers many concrete examples of the sorts of skills and social practices that are reflective of racial literacy: learning about the history of racism in our country; becoming media literate and building the capacity to identify and challenge racist images; being willing to tolerate discomfort associated with honest discussions of about racism and racial privilege; acknowledging ourselves as racial beings with limited perspectives on race; striving for humility and being willing to not know; and taking antiracist action.

CRT Influences Conceptions of Whiteness

CRT also informs the ways we understand Whiteness. Whiteness, like race generally, is a social construct. Whiteness is neither objective nor biological but arbitrary and malleable. What it means to be White has changed over time and varies in different parts of the world. White people have invented and adapted Whiteness, using it to justify social inequality based on race. As such, Whiteness operates materially as White privilege, which describes a system of unearned advantages from which White people benefit (Frankenberg, 1993; Lipsitz, 2006; McIntosh, 1989).

Because Whiteness maintains power, in part, through maintaining invisibility, one of the main goals of antiracist education is making Whiteness visible. Naming it and calling out the ways it works helps to deconstruct Whiteness as a category, delegitimize its neutrality, and reveal the ways it operates as an ideology. In White-dominant contexts, this work often begins with providing opportunities for students to reflect on their own racial identities and experiences, for examining taken for granted assumptions about themselves and others.

WHAT IS ANTIRACIST LITERATURE INSTRUCTION AND WHY TAKE IT UP?

Many English teachers have a strong desire to be more antiracist in their literature instruction, but what might that look like? Our book presents *antiracist literature instruction*, a framework we have designed that merges antiracist goals together with familiar tools for literature instruction. In the chapters that follow, we flesh out a range of concrete examples intended to guide English teachers in their efforts to address racism through literature in White schools.

To start, antiracist literature instruction makes race and racism a central and explicit part of curriculum and instruction by foregrounding racial literacy goals as they relate to literature learning specifically, such as:

- identifying examples of racism in literature and the world as operating on individual, institutional, sociological, and/or epistemological levels
- understanding race concepts, such as colorblindness, White privilege, racial identity, White savior complex, and so on, and using those concepts in literary interpretations
- considering one's own racial identity and how that racial identity influences one's interpretations of literature
- using literature as a platform from which to engage in talk about race and racism even when it is difficult, awkward, or uncomfortable
- leveraging understandings of race and racism in literature into an ability to name and challenge forms of everyday racism in the world
- recognizing the role literature plays in reinforcing or interrupting constructions of race and racial stereotypes

In Chapter 2, we offer resources for thinking about how to articulate racial literacy objectives, questions, and assessments to guide literature-based units.

Antiracist literature instruction builds students' vocabulary around race and racism and helps them apply their understandings to interpretations of literary texts. In Chapter 2 we sketch out one example to show how learning about the concept of societal racism can open up students' understanding of racism, as well as their interpretations of a key literary text.

Of course, knowing that antiracist teaching and learning gets done through the texts that we teach, and knowing that literature curriculum has traditionally overrepresented Whiteness, antiracist literature instruction prioritizes literature featuring authors and characters of color in myriad rich, complex, and celebratory ways. In Chapter 3, we lay out antiracist principles for selecting texts.

In some cases, the racism English teachers want to interrupt is circulated in the racist ideologies of literary texts themselves. Antiracist literature instruction equips students to critically analyze those texts to expose dominant racial ideologies. In Chapters 4 and 5, we illustrate methods for analyzing literature from a critical race perspective.

Antiracist literature instruction provides students opportunities to engage in open and honest discussions about the nature and implications of racism. In Chapter 6, we outline a range of proactive and reactive strategies for facilitating whole group conversations about race, racism, and Whiteness.

Reflecting on one's own racial positioning is central to racial literacy for White students. Antiracist literature instruction includes opportunities for students to apply their developing understandings of race and racism to their own lives and experiences. In Chapter 7, we offer examples of the kinds of assessments English teachers can design to scaffold White students' racial identities and literacies through writing.

To be clear, antiracist literature instruction does not position literature as a tool in the service of racial literacy goals only. Rather, we see the relationship between goals of racial literacy and the goals of typical literature instruction as being mutually beneficial. While we see literature as a platform for helping students to build their racial literacies, we also see the complex understandings that come with racial literacy development as leading to deeper interpretations of literature.

Of course, the examples we lay out throughout the book are not the only ways to do antiracist literature instruction. In fact, we see strong parallels between our work and others in our field who are also leveraging literature for antiracist goals (e.g., Butler, 2017; Rogers & Mosley, 2006). We think of antiracist literature instruction as an example of L. L. Johnson's (2018) critical race English education (CREE), a framework for reimagining English curriculum and instruction in response to racial violence and anti-Blackness. CREE "seeks to dismantle dominant texts (i.e., canonical texts, art, and media texts) while also highlighting how language and literacy can be used as tools to uplift the lives of people who are often on the margins in society and PreK–20 spaces" (p. 108). While Johnson focuses primarily on achieving these goals through his work with Black youth, we see ourselves as approaching the problem from the other side of the same coin by interrupting racism through literature instruction with White students.

NOTES ON AUTHORIAL DECISIONS

We made some decisions about our focus in this book, about how we would present ideas, as well as how we would both protect the anonymity of participants and give credit to teachers and students comfortable with having us share their writing. Next, we explain some of these decisions to guide your reading.

A Focus on Black and White

Readers will notice that throughout the book we have framed race in Black and White racial terms. To be clear, our focus on Blackness and Whiteness is not intended to ignore or silence other minoritized groups' experiences with oppression. CRT itself, while it speaks to the experiences of all people of color to some degree, grows specifically out of the historical legacy and present-day experiences of African Americans in the United States. In fact, more specific theories—LatCrit, TribalCrit, AsianCrit—have developed under the umbrella of CRT to speak to the particular concerns of Latinx, Indigenous and American Indian, and Asian American communities. Each of these theories recognizes all oppression as intertwined, while also addressing the unique challenges facing particular communities.

We acknowledge that this decision to focus on Blackness and Whiteness risks reinforcing limited notions of race and racism in terms of a Black/White binary. At the same time, however, one of the challenges we have faced with our own students is helping them to reach the depth of understanding necessary for fully grasping the complexities of systemic racism. Building that understanding requires us to dig deeply into the particulars of historical and present-day examples. Therefore, we opted to focus intensively on race and racism as they apply to Blackness and Whiteness in the United States as opposed to covering race and racism as they apply to people of color more generally.

Finally, our focus on Blackness and Whiteness also reflects, in part, the Black/White binary we see in much commonly taught literature. As Morrison (1992) argues, Whiteness in American literature has been defined, in large part, in contrast to Blackness. In *Playing in the Dark*, she illustrates her argument through an analysis of Poe, Hemingway, Twain, and others. This particular construction of Whiteness in contrast to Blackness speaks to challenges many English teachers face in trying to do justice to commonly taught texts, such as *To Kill a Mockingbird* and *Adventures of Huckleberry Finn*, for example. Our choice to focus on Blackness and Whiteness reflects an effort to address challenges rooted in teaching particular commonly taught texts.

Implicating Ourselves in Discussions of White Teachers, Students, and Classroom Practices

Every chapter includes scenes and examples from secondary and university classrooms. In these scenes, we reference the work of White teachers and students and the kinds of problems teachers might expect when attempting to address racism in White contexts. We include these examples—including scenes in our own classrooms and from our own experiences—not to put the blame on White teachers, teacher candidates, or students. Rather, we offer such specific scenes and examples to help readers recognize these problems to better unpack them from an antiracist perspective. Our aim is not to traipse upon the genuine efforts made by teachers to do this work, but to help all of us do this work better. You will notice that as we write about White teachers and students, we try to use "we" as often as possible to implicate ourselves in critiques of Whiteness, even as we lay out the principles and practice of antiracist literature instruction throughout this book.

Additionally, we know that our Whiteness has shaped our writing of this book in many ways that both benefit and limit the project. In some ways, Whiteness can be an asset in antiracist teaching with White students and teachers. For example, we can draw on our own experiences to relate to our students and model what the process might look like for them. Also, because we are White, we are aware of some of the concerns that are preventing White teachers from doing this work, concerns that we make visible throughout this book to help other White teachers see themselves in this process.

On the other hand, because we are White, we have not always pushed students as hard toward antiracist practices, drawing on the privilege of choosing when and how to address racism. Thus, although we have *considered* ourselves aligned with antiracist goals for a long time, and although we have done work on racism in our teaching and scholarship, only recently have we both pushed *much* harder to effect changes in the ways teachers are being prepared in our institutions with respect to antiracist goals. To do so, together we began to read research and scholarship by and about people of color so that we could discuss the readings together, considering implications for our teaching. We staged a semester-long research study across our two institutions focusing on strategies that might help preservice White teachers take on antiracist goals in their future classrooms. We participated in workshops and conference presentations and joined efforts on our campuses to challenge racism in our institutions. Still, we acknowledge the difference between *choosing* this work as White scholars versus the experiences of our colleagues of color for whom it is not optional. In writing this book as White women, we know that we remain vulnerable to ideological blindnesses stemming from our racial privileges.

Names and Identities

All examples in the book come from real teachers and real classrooms—from data collection through surveys, interviews, and classroom observations we have conducted in formal research, as well as anecdotes we have gathered through personal communication over the past 15 years. When we name teachers in the book, the use of only a first name signals that we are utilizing a pseudonym to protect anonymity; the use of a full name signals that we have gotten permission to do so.

We have written this book with the needs and interests of secondary English teachers and English teacher candidates in mind. It is the book we wish we had in our hands when we started teaching. We wrote it to put it into the hands of the many teachers asking us how to do this well. For you, the teachers who pressed us with questions echoing our own—especially when we really weren't sure how to do this work well ourselves yet—we present this book.

CHAPTER 2

Designing Racial Literacy Objectives and Assessments for Literature-Based Units

Antiracist literature instruction does not happen by accident. As with other, meaningful learning goals in the English curriculum, teaching about race and racism via literary study requires deliberate, thoughtful methods. One of the ways that we, as English teachers, can ensure that we are addressing race and racism responsibly is by designing literature curriculum that includes objectives and assessments that prioritize racial literacy goals. In this chapter, we discuss the need for clear, race-based unit objectives and assessments in antiracist literature instruction.

COMMON CHALLENGE: GLOSSING OVER COMPLEX RACE CONCEPTS

Sometime in April, Ms. Kinney brought a cartoon featuring Obama as Bugs Bunny (see Figure 2.1) into her 9th-grade English classroom during their study of *A Raisin in the Sun*. The cartoon, which was created by Victor Juhasz in 2008 and published in *Rolling Stone*, focuses on the presidential campaign of 2008, when Barack Obama and Joe Biden ran against John McCain and Sarah Palin.

Ms. Kinney introduced the cartoon to open a discussion of "racism today" and make the point that racism is not a thing of the past. In this exchange, Ms. Kinney, a teacher in her 14th year of teaching, also discussed a trip to Cuba taken with another teacher from the school, Mr. Smith. The school is a predominantly White, high-performing high school in the Midwest. The following exchange took place during a whole-group discussion after Ms. Kinney asked, "What is this cartoon saying?"

> *Ms. Kinney:* Speaking of Obama. This was a cartoon that showed up during the campaign. Who are the Elmer Fudds?
> *Students:* McCain and Palin.

Figure 2.1. Obama as Bugs Bunny

> *Ms. Kinney:* McCain and Palin. Now look at this picture and think,
> what is this picture trying to say? And we may overanalyze it but . .
> . . Do you know the Bugs Bunny cartoon?
> *Molly:* Isn't it that Bugs Bunny is always like clever and fooling Elmer
> Fudd and the other person? He fools the hunters all the time.
> *Ms. Kinney:* Yeah, they're supposed to be Elmer Fudd, who is the idiot
> who Bugs Bunny always outwits, or whatever. I think we could
> definitely say that this is negative about McCain and Palin, um, but
> why could it also be negative about Obama? This is what Mr. Smith
> would argue.
> *Jason:* Trying to trick people.
> *Ms. Kinney:* Yeah, and there were often pictures of the African
> American trying to be the trickster, um, you know, outwitting
> people, being the sly one. And then, um, it's also interesting that
> they end up in blackface. What is blackface? Have you heard
> about that? When actors or comedians or dancers would put black
> make-up on their face when they were pretending to be, um, of
> African American race and it was a very offensive thing? We were

just on vacation, this is so funny, we were just on vacation. We had the TV on and there was this Cuban station—and we love Cuba, you know. And so we were watching—and if you ever watch those stations, they're like back into the 70s. It's really funny. There's this Cuban dance show and there were a couple people in blackface and we were like, "Oh my god, they're in blackface." You know, so sometimes it happens even today.

Brandon: I'm pretty sure they're in blackface because of the gunpowder.

Ms. Kinney: Well, right, of course, but you could argue, what is that saying? It's because of the gunpowder of course.

Brandon: I know but like you can draw anything now and people will find a way to think that it's racist.

Ms. Kinney: Absolutely. You could look at this and argue that it's not racist because they're the ones who look like idiots. You could take it either way.

WHY THIS MATTERS FROM AN ANTIRACIST PERSPECTIVE

One of the reasons we love this example from Ms. Kinney's classroom is that it is indicative of common challenges we have faced, especially with White students. Unpacking this example helps us to understand problems we see with the outcome of this lesson for the purpose of improving our own practice. Next, we discuss what worked and what did not in this teaching scenario from an antiracist perspective.

There is much to applaud in Ms. Kinney's efforts to address racism in the midst of her literature unit. We would note that *not* talking about racism today in the context of a unit like this may contribute to colorblindness and exacerbate the invisibility of racism for many White students. Ms. Kinney was proactive in responding to the fact that many White students often consider racism to be a problem of the past. Her idea to bring in an artifact from popular culture that raises contemporary race questions as part of their *A Raisin in the Sun* unit was insightful.

At the same time, however, by framing the discussion as potential "overanalysis," rather than a straightforward analysis of what is visible in the image, Ms. Kinney delegitimized the critical race analysis from the get-go. Her framing of the activity as potential overanalysis permitted responses that were framed as a matter of opinion. Ms. Kinney suggested that students who agreed with the emerging critical race analysis could be seen as overly sensitive rather than engaging in legitimate critique.

In terms of strengths, in her efforts to extend students' analysis of the cartoon, Ms. Kinney demonstrated racial literacy knowledge related to the significant role rabbit tricksters have played in African American culture.

She helped students notice how the portrayal of President Obama as Bugs Bunny characterized him as an example of a trickster figure. Here, her reference to the rabbit trickster is tied to work in literary studies that often traces Bugs Bunny back to Brer Rabbit. In Uncle Remus stories, Brer Rabbit, the seemingly weaker species, uses his cunning and wit to not only triumph over his opponent, often a fox, but also make a fool of the fox in the process. In the African American tradition, the trickster character has represented a form of symbolic protest through story: The (White) fox is replaced by the (Black) rabbit; the fox becomes the dupe; the hunter becomes the hunted (Wolfe, 1949). In other words, the power dynamic is flipped. As Ms. Kinney suggested, knowledge of trickster characters is essential to a deeper interpretation of this layered and very complex cartoon.

Yet, Ms. Kinney only briefly glossed over this complex concept, leaving it as a mention rather than a topic worthy of deep understanding. Given her students' lack of familiarity with the concept, referencing it swiftly, without explanation, undermines Ms. Kinney's commitment to really teaching about it. Difficult and/or new concepts, especially concepts that run counter to dominant thinking, require deliberate scaffolding so that they will "stick" for students.

To reach a deeper analysis, Ms. Kinney might have probed a bit further, leading students to connect Bugs Bunny to Brer Rabbit and to the racial dynamics of the Obama campaign. For example, this Bugs Bunny cartoon, with roots in African American folktales and referencing Obama, certainly evokes commentary on the racial dynamics of the 2008 presidential election. Recognizing Obama as the rabbit trickster in the cartoon invites viewers to see him as a wily force against the White "hunters" attempting to bring him down. Through this rendering, students might have interpreted the cartoon as suggestive of an inversion of racial power dynamics in the campaign.

Similarly, Ms. Kinney raised another complex racial topic when she suggested that the gunpowder on the Fudds' faces might be construed as blackface. Blackface refers to a tradition of White individuals painting their faces and performing in minstrel shows, a tradition that draws upon racist stereotypes of Black people. Rather than offering this history, however, Ms. Kinney references an example of blackface that she personally saw on Cuban television as funny, a point she repeated twice as she described the televised images. By repeating how "funny" it was, Ms. Kinney temporarily joined other racist White viewers enjoying such portrayals of mocked Black people, at the same time that her stated aims set out to interrupt such racist thinking. It's possible that her attempt at humor was aimed at dispelling discomfort in the room, but in the end the connection between blackface and the cartoon seemed to be lost.

Ms. Kinney might have led students to analyze the relationship between blackface and the presidential election. For example, by depicting McCain and Palin as wearing blackface in their "performances" during the campaign, the cartoonist may have been signaling to knowledgeable viewers that these politicians are relying on racist stereotypes to be elected. But these characters are no minstrels; they have been *tricked* into "performing" in blackface. In other words, Obama—the hunted—cleverly exposes the racism that McCain and Palin—the hunters—rely upon in the campaign. Once again, Juhasz may be suggesting an inversion of contemporary American racial dynamics.

In the end, when Ms. Kinney faced resistance from Brandon to the suggestion that the cartoon referenced blackface, she backed down from the analysis, agreeing that it could be argued differently. By agreeing to his comment, she reinforced the message that it is [overly sensitive] viewers who bring such readings *into* interpretations rather than the other way around. When Ms. Kinney closed this lesson with the words "you can take it either way," she left the door open for her students to ignore the complex messages about race to which she attempted to expose them through the cartoon. In the end, the lesson frames race issues in terms of individual opinions, rather than concepts to be learned and understood.

What can we take from this example to help us understand our own practice? What is the common challenge at the heart of this scenario? In our eyes, Ms. Kinney saw a need to address racism with her students, but she seemed ambivalent about carrying out her lesson related to analyzing race in the political cartoon. In the remaining sections of this chapter, we argue that the familiar pedagogical principle of backward design might support teachers like Ms. Kinney in being more confident and purposeful in their teaching about race and racism. For example, what was it that Ms. Kinney wanted her students to know or be able to do with regard to racism? What connection did she see between this cartoon and their study of *A Raisin in the Sun*? How might Ms. Kinney plan to tie her goals for teaching about racism to other learning goals in this literature unit?

WHAT YOU CAN DO: USE BACKWARD PLANNING TO DESIGN LITERATURE UNITS FOR RACIAL LITERACY

In response to this common problem of taking on the teaching of racism without a clear curricular roadmap or set of objectives, we encourage English teachers to return to a familiar pedagogical principle that undergirds effective teaching about any topic: backward design (Wiggins & McTighe, 2005). Backward design is an approach to planning curricular units based on the idea that curriculum design should start with the end in mind by articulating goals and objectives. With goals for student learning in place, teachers then work backward to pose essential questions to engage students and then design assessments that match those objectives, before turning to thinking about how specific lessons help to scaffold student learning toward

COMMON CONCERNS RELATED TO TEACHING ABOUT RACISM

While this chapter—and the entire book—foregrounds strategies teachers can use in their classrooms to address racism, we also discuss some of the emotional and psychological reasons that the "Common Challenges" we feature in each chapter are so common. In this chapter, Ms. Kinney's example helps us all understand why it might be that some teachers struggle to address racism effectively despite the desire to do so. Recognizing such contradictory drives—of wanting to teach about racism but feeling afraid of doing so—helps us to face them and then move beyond them to achieve antiracist goals. Here are some of the common concerns that we have heard Ms. Kinney and other White English teachers express.

Losing Rapport

As English teachers who spend so much time establishing rapport with students to secure student buy-in to the rigors of curriculum, introducing the discomforts of learning about White people's role in racism could not be further from what we want to be doing. Teachers who intend to initiate lessons on race end up wondering, "What will happen to my relationships with students if I offend them, make them feel defensive, or make them feel bad?" This comment may have less to do with not wanting to talk about racism and more to do with the fact that pushing against students' assumptions about racism can feel threatening to the otherwise warm relationships teachers work so hard to build. When we have experienced the kind of resistance that Ms. Kinney encountered from Brandon, we have sometimes felt reluctant to push back on that resistance because we have worried about shutting students down and threatening the "safe" learning environment we toiled so hard to establish.

That said, when teachers skirt the topic of racism to avoid threatening the "safe" classroom environment, we must ask ourselves several questions: What message are we sending other students when we back down from one student's racism? Whose voices and perspectives are given priority? What about students who are eager to engage with us in serious antiracist work? Whose safety are we most concerned about? Moreover, even in predominantly White teaching contexts, we must ask ourselves, To what extent are we considering the safety of the few students of color? Additionally, what are the effects of asking students of color, who are the minority in White-dominant settings, to sit through discussions like these in our classrooms? What are the effects of consuming texts like *A Raisin in the Sun,* texts intended to confront racism, without a rigorous social critique emphasized through our teaching? These decisions have implications for all students.

COMMON CONCERNS RELATED TO TEACHING ABOUT RACISM, CONTINUED

Remaining Politically Neutral

For some of us, broaching the topic of racism in class feels as though we are crossing a political line, allowing our personal politics to affect a teaching environment intended for students from families with a range of political opinions. Many English teachers feel that they are supposed to keep their thoughts and opinions to themselves (Leer, 2010). Yet, we know that the teaching of English content has never been devoid of politics. The literature we teach evokes these political conversations. It would be impossible, for example, to read *A Raisin in the Sun* in a politically neutral way. Engaging directly with the topic of racism in *A Raisin in the Sun* may be perceived as a political choice, but *not* engaging directly with the topic of racism in *A Raisin in the Sun* is also a political choice. Not engaging directly with racism may *seem* less political. However, we would argue that teaching a subversive text without consideration of its social critique not only dishonors the text but also functions as a perpetuation of the very racism that text was written to affect. In short, all decisions that English teachers make are political: Both the questions we ask and the questions we do not ask teach lessons about race and racism.

Losing Sight of English Content

Some teachers fear that addressing racism veers too far away from "English" content. Traditional literature instruction, as it has been practiced in many English classrooms for many years (Applebee, 1993), has been informed loosely by a New Critical approach, emphasizing interpretations of literature based on form, structure, and the inherent meaning of a text without as much focus on the sociohistorical context. In practice, a traditional New Critical approach, which often looks like close readings of text with a focus on literary devices, like theme, symbol, and character development, may feel "neutral" because it is easily recognizable as typical in many high school classrooms. From this perspective, teaching about racism may seem to some to go beyond the purview of what English teachers are tasked to do.

In recent years, however, English educators have argued that teaching students to understand the ideological nature of literature—in all texts—is exactly what literature instruction should do. Scholars promoting critical race English education (L. L. Johnson, 2018), critical literature pedagogy (Borsheim-Black, Macaluso, & Petrone, 2014; Dyches, 2018; Macaluso, 2017), and critical literary study (Appleman, 2015), for example, have emphasized the power of literature as a platform from which to prepare students to read not only the *word* but also the *world* (Freire, 1970). Interrogating problematic racial ideologies of canonical texts like *Adventures of Huckleberry Finn*

COMMON CONCERNS RELATED TO TEACHING ABOUT RACISM, CONTINUED

by Mark Twain; delving deeply into the antiracist themes in *Beloved* by Toni Morrison; discussing legacies of historical racism in contemporary young adult literature, like *Monster* by Walter Dean Myers; reflecting on Whiteness and institutional racism in texts shaping the contemporary discourse around racism, such as *Between the World and Me* by Ta-Nehisi Coates. What could be more squarely within what English teachers hope to do in their classrooms?

Losing Control of the Conversation

Many teachers worry about what could happen when they raise the topic of racism. They worry that they do not have a sophisticated enough understanding of racism themselves and therefore will feel ill-prepared to respond to difficult questions. They worry about discussions becoming heated or unpredictable. They worry that students will disagree with one another and that disagreements about racism in class could further fuel already-existing racial tension or further cement students' racist thinking. They worry that the conversation may single out or silence students of color.

We would like to validate these feelings. We have sometimes fallen back on race-evasive practices in our own teaching, and we still sometimes do when we set out to do this work anew in a fresh setting. In fact, research, as well as our observations in many classrooms, suggests that this scenario is common and indicative of the kinds of challenges that many, many English teachers face (e.g., Lewis et al., 2001; Thomas, 2015). At the same time, we also know these fears, uncertainties, and ambivalent feelings can sabotage English teachers' efforts to teach about racism before they even begin (e.g., Borsheim-Black, 2018). In other words, each of these concerns must be faced if teachers are to more successfully delve into the work of teaching about racism.

In the remaining sections of this chapter, we argue that overcoming uncertain feelings begins with articulating a clear sense of purpose. Only when teachers treat racial literacy goals the way we treat other complex literature-based goals will we begin to see the kinds of shifts in racial literacy that antiracist teachers aim to effect. We argue that deliberate planning—concrete objectives and assessments tied closely to the literature—can help English teachers meet uncertainties with sustained and strategic instruction.

those ends (Wiggins & McTighe, 2005). From Wiggins and McTighe, we take three main principles and apply them to racial literacy learning in the context of literature-based units.

Principle 1: Articulate Racial Literacy Objectives

The first principle of backward design is to articulate student learning objectives. We argue that this principle should be applied to teaching about racism via literature study. In our experience, clear, explicit racial literacy goals are not common in literature study. In fact, in a series of surveys and interviews that Carlin conducted, English teachers often framed their goals of teaching about racism in terms of *exposing* students to multiple points of view. English teachers talked about addressing the topic of racism as a sort of by-product of whole-group discussion, explaining that they address it "when it comes up" or as it "emerges" in discussion. "Exposing" students to whole-group discussion about complex race concepts does not ensure that student understanding is carefully introduced, scaffolded, practiced, and assessed. Skerrett (2011) calls this approach to teaching racial literacy an "incidental" approach, citing it as ineffective as a strategy for meeting antiracist goals. Skerrett finds that English teachers need a "sustained and strategic" focus across curricula if complex racial literacy goals are to be met. Clear racial literacy objectives not only guide sustained and strategic instruction; they serve several other purposes as well.

Race-Based Objectives Zero In on Specific Race Concepts. The topic of racism can seem broad and overwhelming. Ms. Kinney's original goal was for students "to understand that racism is not a thing of the past." But, tackling the broad topic of "racism today" as it relates to the main text or the cartoon could take students anywhere from the role of racism in the legal or housing system to complex understandings of Black identities to tricksters to blackface to the Obama campaign. Each of these concepts is complex, requiring depth of knowledge on the part of the teacher, as well as sustained and deliberate instruction for students. Identifying one or two key race concepts closely tied to the literary text proves helpful for narrowing the topic and making it more manageable for a single literature unit for both English teachers and students.

Race-Based Objectives Tie Racial Literacy Directly to Literature Learning. At times, we have heard some teachers ask, "But I teach English. Doesn't this go beyond what I am supposed to do?" "What if students, parents, colleagues, or administrators question a focus on racism in literary study? How do I make the case for this focus?" Tying racial literacy objectives closely to literary analysis—and arguing that deep understanding of these race-related concepts is crucial for deep understanding of the literature—is one way we have learned to make the case to others. From this perspective, the question becomes, How could we possibly teach *A Raisin in the Sun* and *not* address complex race concepts?

Race-Based Objectives Frame Racism as a Concept to Be Learned Rather Than an Opinion to Be Changed. Some approaches to antiracist education prioritize instruction that challenges students' beliefs and assumptions. While we recognize that reflecting on students' personal beliefs is incredibly important, we would argue that there are some aspects to understanding racism that are not a matter of opinion. There are basic concepts, like systemic racism, for example, that have nothing to do with opinion, regardless of how some political positions render such facts. Conceiving of racial literacy in this way offers a path forward for framing race concepts that teachers can teach and students can learn.

Principle 2: Design Essential Questions Focused on Race

As Wiggins and McTighe (2005) and others argue, well-designed essential questions focus inquiry, learning, and discussion both for the teacher and for students (e.g., Burke, 2010; Smagorinsky, 2007; Wilhelm, 2007). Essential questions are recursive, returning across sites and temporal spaces, and shifting in different sociopolitical contexts. As such, they are considered worthy of an adult's knowledge base and of deep understanding (Wiggins & McTighe, 2005). Good essential questions are open-ended rather than leading; terse and easy to remember; and characterized by "intellectual bite" so that they capture students' imaginations (Traver, 1998). Essential questions help to focus a literary unit that explores racism, and they could help teachers consider how to strategically begin *and* sustain (Skerrett, 2011) such race-based studies across curriculum.

When working to identify strong essential questions related to literary texts, English teachers can ask: What question directs us to complex ideas about race and racism in this text and in the world? What question will guide our inquiry of facets of race and racism featured in this text? We make suggestions for potential questions related to *A Raisin in the Sun* later in this chapter.

Principle 3: Assess Racial Literacy Objectives

With clear racial literacy learning objectives and essential and guiding questions in place, a backward design approach to curriculum now requires teachers to shape assessments that match those objectives. In secondary literature study, assessments related to literature often ask students to analyze theme, symbol, or character development in a literary analysis paper or related project. In our own research, however, assessment in literary study rarely addresses what students have learned in terms of racial literacy.

Assessments generally do not ask students to address their understanding of race concepts or the application of those concepts to literary analysis. We believe that adding this dimension to curriculum design—tying learning goals and even grades to racial literacy growth—can have a potent impact on student learning around race.

At this point in the process, English teachers can look to the key race concepts, the racial literacy objectives, and the essential questions for direction on a summative assessment that makes sense for the unit goals and purposes. English teachers can ask:

- How can students demonstrate the extent to which they know and can apply key race concepts?
- How can students demonstrate their racial literacy learning?

As it is conventionally understood, literary assessment may seem distant from efforts to effect antiracist learning, like considering their own taken-for-granted racial assumptions. But we know that it can be hard for a teacher to determine whether students have "learned" such racial content on a personal level. Additionally, students can "mimic" antiracist discourse from a personal standpoint that does not tie to deep understandings of the complexities around racism. To be clear, this personal work is imperative for helping students challenge deeply held assumptions and develop healthy racial identities, and the journey of self-discovery will take a lifetime of committed effort for all White students. However, it is very difficult to evaluate this process in any fair way. Identifying concepts and articulating objectives makes it possible to assess student learning and growth around racial literacy. In fact, we argue that assessing racial literacy accomplishes two important things.

Assessing Racial Literacy Moves Racial Literacy to the Center. Even if teachers identify learning objectives and essential questions specific to racial literacy and assign complementary content to extend student learning around racism, our curriculum sends contradictory messages to students if racial literacy is omitted from assessment. Assessing students' growth in racial literacy sends a message to students that this content is important, and that they are accountable for learning it.

Assessing Racial Literacy Informs Subsequent Practice. When assessment follows the path set up by objectives and essential questions, teachers will have data from students' work documenting the extent to which students have deeply understood this important material. Accordingly, teachers will be able to study these assessment data to determine which facets of the curriculum prove easier for students to understand and which pose greater challenges, so that teachers can continue to hone their practices toward these goals.

IN THE CLASSROOM: ARTICULATING RACIAL LITERACY
OBJECTIVES FOR *A RAISIN IN THE SUN*

In this section, we apply the principles outlined above to design a unit around *A Raisin in the Sun*.

Racial Literacy Objectives to Guide a Unit on *A Raisin in the Sun*

Here we turn our attention from the specific cartoon referenced in our anecdote above to develop sample objectives, questions, and assessments for a broader unit of study focused on the main text, *A Raisin in the Sun*, an award-winning play by Lorraine Hansberry, which debuted on Broadway in 1959. The play depicts the experiences of the Youngers, a Black family comprising Mama, her children Beneatha and Walter, Walter's wife Ruth, and their son Travis, as they contemplate what to do with insurance money they will receive following the death of Mama's husband. Although they all have ideas about how the $10,000 might help them out of poverty and their one-room apartment in a southside Chicago neighborhood, one of the main plotlines centers around Mama's decision to put money down on a house in an all-White neighborhood.

To begin the process of articulating racial literacy objectives, we first identified key race concepts that are central to understanding the literary text by asking ourselves: *What race concepts do students need to know in order to fully appreciate this text?* Starting with the title's reference to Langston Hughes's poem "Harlem," the play explores many race-related themes. Walter's character struggles with the frustration of limited opportunity and a lifetime of thwarted aspirations. Beneatha's character explores her identity and weighs the limitations of assimilation against embracing her African roots. To narrow our focus in this case, we directed our attention to a pivotal moment in the story, an example of overt racial discrimination that occurs when the Younger family, in the face of realizing their dream of owning a home, are confronted by a White neighbor, Karl Lindner, who tries to bribe them out of the neighborhood in order to maintain segregation:

> *Lindner:* Yes—that's the way we feel out in Clybourne Park. And that's why I was elected to come here this afternoon and talk to you people. Friendly like, you know, the way people should talk to each other and see if we couldn't find some way to work this thing out. As I say, the whole business is a matter of caring about the other fellow. Anybody can see that you are a nice family of folks, hard-working and honest I'm sure. Today everybody knows what it means to be on the outside of something. And of course, there is always somebody who is out to take advantage of people who don't always understand.

Walter: What do you mean?

Lindner: Well—you see our community is made up of people who've worked hard as the dickens for years to build up that little community. They're not rich and fancy people; just hard-working, honest people who don't really have much but those little homes and a dream of the kind of community they want to raise their children in. Now, I don't say we are perfect and there is a lot wrong in some of the things they want. But you've got to admit that a man, right or wrong, has the right to want to have the neighborhood he lives in a certain kind of way. And at the moment the overwhelming majority of our people out there feel that people get along better, take more of a common interest in the life of the community, when they share a common background. I want you to believe me when I tell you that race prejudice simply doesn't enter into it. It is a matter of the people of Clybourne Park believing, rightly or wrongly, as I say, that for the happiness of all concerned that our Negro families are happier when they live in their own communities.

Beneatha (with a grand and bitter gesture): This, friends, is the Welcoming Committee!

As we read this excerpt, we asked ourselves, what key race concepts does this scene expose that require unpacking? We were struck by the fact that this scene exemplifies ways that racism works overtly and covertly on multiple levels—individual, institutional, and societal (e.g., Scheurich & Young, 1997). Individual racism describes overt and covert acts of racial discrimination. In this case, Lindner and other neighbors personally discriminate against the Youngers in an effort to maintain segregation.

Asking students to spot this evidence of individual racism within this example is a pretty typical move in teaching *A Raisin in the Sun*. However, we would argue that it does not substantially stretch students' racial literacy *or* fully capture the complexity of this scene. What other key race concepts does this scene evoke? This question pointed us to the concept of *institutional racism*, which describes instances when institutions—through laws, citizenship, education, and so on—have standard operating procedures that marginalize members of one or more races, while privileging members of the dominant race (Scheurich & Young, 1997). Naming the concept of institutional racism also would help students understand the personal experiences that Hansberry's family had with housing discrimination in the 1930s in Chicago when they were evicted from their home as a result of a racially restrictive covenant, a legal protection that prevented ownership or occupancy by Blacks. Carl Hansberry, Lorraine's father, sued and the case went all the way to the Supreme Court. With an understanding of institutional racism, students could make the connection between the neighborhood association in this excerpt, which is not acting in accordance with any formal policy or law, and the case with the Hansberry family, where there was a legal covenant. Thus, the play illustrates ways that White people have worked covertly to achieve the same goals—in ways that still have material consequences for Black families.

This passage pointed us to another key race concept: *White privilege.* Understanding this aspect of Hansberry's play depends on students understanding that White privilege has operated in the United States through ownership, property values, and the accumulation and distribution of generational wealth. For example, ownership and property values have been protected for White people and thwarted for African American people for generations, sometimes through laws like restrictive covenants, sometimes through policies like redlining, and sometimes through individual actions like White flight or refusing to rent to people of color.

Even beyond institutional racism, there is more happening in Lindner's comments that is important to understand. Why and how does Lindner try to persuade the Youngers not to move to his neighborhood, while also trying not to appear overtly racist? To get at this point, students also need to understand the key race concept of *societal racism*, which refers to the ways prevailing cultural assumptions, norms, concepts, habits, and expectations favor one race over one or more other races (Scheurich & Young, 1997). On a societal level, Lindner's rationale for trying to buy the Youngers out of purchasing a home in a White neighborhood reflects *colorblindness*, a dominant racial ideology that functions to maintain the racial status quo of inequity while seemingly rendering the White speaker reasonable rather than racist. As Bonilla-Silva (2013) explains, White people who may not consider themselves racist consistently take up four central frames of colorblind ideology. In this excerpt, Lindner takes up the central frame of *abstract liberalism*, which picks up tenets of liberalism, like individualism and meritocracy, and applies them in "abstract" ways to uphold racist practices. How does Lindner exhibit elements of colorblindness to distance himself from appearing overtly racist? When Lindner defends his effort to bribe the Youngers, a move intended to uphold racial housing segregation, he does so by asserting that he and his White neighbors are "not rich and fancy people; just hard-working, honest people who don't really have much but those little homes and a dream of the kind of community they want to raise their children in." Lindner draws from the abstract liberal principle of meritocracy—"just hard-working, honest people"—to reinforce their White "honesty" rather than racism.

Similarly, Lindner also draws from the central frame of *naturalization*, which, Bonilla-Silva (2013) explains, renders current race relations as "natural" rather than the result of historical and continued racist practices, suggesting that racism is just the way things are. So, when Lindner suggests that he and his White neighbors are supporting "happiness" through this attempted bribery by affirming that "our Negro families are happier when they live in their own communities," he takes up the frame of naturalization rather than expose his own active White efforts to maintain strict racial segregation. Again, applying the concept of colorblindness to literary analysis not only deepens students' understanding of the complexity of Hansberry's play, but also equips them to recognize similar examples in our society today.

Once we identified key race concepts, our next step was to use those concepts to articulate racial literacy objectives that connected types of racism in the play to types of racism still circulating in other texts and the world today. For our *A Raisin in the Sun* unit, we suggest the following objectives:

- Students will be able to name ways racism works on individual, institutional, and societal levels in *A Raisin in the Sun* and in their own lives.
- Students will be able to understand central frames of colorblind racial ideology in literature and in society.

These objectives, of course, would not be the only ones framing a unit on *A Raisin in the Sun*. These racial literacy objectives could work in concert with other, more traditional objectives for reading and analyzing literature, such as those outlined by the Common Core State Standards. At the same time, however, we argue that traditional objectives alone often do not translate to deliberate teaching about race and racism in the context of typical literature instruction, as illustrated by Ms. Kinney's example above.

We hope this example underscores our argument that understanding important race-related concepts is integral to full and deep analysis of literature. In this case, naming types of racism offers possibilities for deep understanding of one of the central points Hansberry is trying to make. Moreover, such learning objectives instantly infuse a text like Hansberry's with robust contemporary relevance and prepare students to recognize comparable examples in their own lives as well. Without understanding types of racism, how would students be able to appreciate the full historical and contemporary impact of Lorraine Hansberry's work? Without an understanding of the role colorblindness plays in contemporary discourse, might students miss important opportunities to connect literature to their lives? Without the analytic rigor of access to racist rhetoric that continues to circulate today, how can students appreciate the nuanced ways in which racist acts and thinking seemingly can be delivered "innocently" by "honest" people?

Framing Essential Questions for *A Raisin in the Sun*

Once we articulated racial literacy objectives, we worked to articulate essential and guiding questions that connected the key race concepts with universal themes or enduring issues in society today. For example, given our focus on race concepts described above, we asked:

ANOTHER SAMPLE UNIT PLAN OVERVIEW

Of course, there is no one "right" way to apply racial literacy objectives to teaching literature, or even to a specific text. Here, we pull the principles of backward design together once again to flesh out another possibility for what a unit might look like in Ms. Kinney's classroom, given her expressed goals of tying students' study of *A Raisin in the Sun* to their lives today.

To contextualize this unit, we will note that in an interview, Ms. Kinney seemed particularly interested in the fact that her community, which is predominantly White, is located in close proximity to a community that is predominantly African American, which is not uncommon in Michigan, one of the most segregated states in the nation. She had a vague sense of the history behind that segregation and made a connection between her immediate context and a main plot point in *A Raisin in the Sun*, which involves Mr. Lindner, a White man, appearing at the Youngers' front door to offer them money to stay out of his White neighborhood. This sample unit plan follows Ms. Kinney's interest in capitalizing on connections between Hansberry's play and students' immediate community.

Housing Segregation in *A Raisin in the Sun* and in Our Community Today

Racial Literacy Objectives

Students will be able to connect Lorraine Hansberry's representation of housing discrimination in *A Raisin in the Sun* in the 1950s to the legacy of similar examples of housing discrimination in their community today.

Essential Question

• What is housing segregation? How does it happen?

Guiding Questions

• Why is our mid-Michigan region so segregated?
• How does knowing about housing segregation affect our interpretation of *A Raisin in the Sun*?
• What does *A Raisin in the Sun* help us understand about our own lives and the role racism has played in our community?

Text Selection

Hansberry, L. (1959/2004). *A raisin in the sun*. New York, NY: Vintage Books.

Supplementary Texts

Hannah-Jones, N. (Reporter). (2015, July 31). The problem we all live with [Audio podcast]. *This American life*. Retrieved from www.thisamericanlife. org/562/the-problem-we-all-live-with-part-one/act-one-0

| ANOTHER SAMPLE UNIT PLAN OVERVIEW, CONTINUED |

Hannah-Jones is a reporter whose work explores school segregation in the United States. This podcast includes Part One and Part Two in which she covers the community fallout when officials desegregated two schools in Normandy, Missouri. The school district borders Ferguson, Missouri, and one of the schools was the alma mater of Michael Brown.

Williams, L. (2008). *From Flint, Michigan to your front door: Tracing the roots of racism in America.* Retrieved from racebridgesstudio.com/from-flint-to-your-front-door-tracing-the-roots-of-racism-in-america/

Williams is an oral storyteller from Flint, Michigan. His oral stories are available as audio-recordings on his website. Readers learn about systemic racism, redlining, and other complex topics as they are woven through highly engaging stories about his own personal life experiences.

Teaching Resources

Chenelle, S., & Fisch, A. (2014, March 13). Text to text: 'A raisin in the sun' and 'discrimination in housing against nonwhites persists quietly.' *New York Times.* Retrieved from learning.blogs.nytimes.com/2014/03/13/text-to-text-a-raisin-in-the-sun-and-discrimination-in-housing-against-nonwhites-persists-quietly/

This unit, which focuses on the theme of housing discrimination in *A Raisin in the Sun*, evolves from the inquiry question: Do we all have the right to buy a home of our own wherever we want?

Christensen, L. (2015). Reading and writing about the roots of gentrification. *English Journal, 105*(2), 15–21.

This article outlines a research unit focused on gentrification in which students learn about the history of their city, Portland, Oregon, through primary source documents and hands-on investigation. The unit includes a consideration of systemic racism that resulted in segregation of neighborhoods.

Assessment

- Conduct a research project to examine particular examples of laws, policies, and unofficial practices that trace the historical evolution of housing segregation in the local area. Compare/contrast types of housing discrimination in the community with that of the play.
- Write a reflection about what the play and Williams's oral story help you understand about your own community.

Essential Question: What is societal racism?
Guiding Questions: How does the way White characters speak
   about housing and hard work affect our interpretations of racism
   in *A Raisin in the Sun*? How does *A Raisin in the Sun* help us
   understand the ways people support racist practices without
   seemingly sounding racist?

We categorize this line of inquiry in *A Raisin in the Sun* as societal racism because it mirrors commentary repeated across everyday conversations,
political discourse, and discourse in other texts. Helping students to see that
the ways that many Whites speak about race support societal racism will
add layers of understanding to their interpretations of Hansberry's play.

Assessing Students' Racial Understanding Related to A Raisin in the Sun

Our next step was to design summative assessments to monitor students'
racial literacy growth. Once again, we returned to the racial literacy objectives, the key concepts, and the essential and guiding questions. Given our
goals and questions, we could imagine racial literacy assessments, such as:

- requiring students to define key race terms, like institutional
  and societal racism, abstract liberalism, naturalization, and
  colorblindness, and asking students to identify key scenes in the
  play where they see such dynamics in action
- asking students to write a personal, reflective essay about what they
  learned about themselves and racism in society through the study of
  types of racism, including colorblindness, and *A Raisin in the Sun*.

CONCLUSION

In this chapter, we have argued for the use of clear, direct racial literacy
objectives and assessments to drive literary study that focuses on race and
racism. We argue that the use of such commonplace curriculum design strategies will help teachers address their own ambivalence about teaching race
via literary study; will help teachers know how to proceed during instruction if they are faced with challenges to such curriculum; and will strengthen
the teaching of literature, especially literature that already features a societal
critique of racism. In the next chapter, we complicate the role of text selection in antiracist literature instruction.

CHAPTER 3

Introducing Racialized Reader Response

In the next three chapters, we consider issues of text selection from two different angles, what our colleague Ernest Morrell (2018) refers to as *different reading* and *reading differently*. In this chapter, we begin with different reading, which means thinking about issues of representation with regard to race across the literature curriculum, reflecting the efforts of recent movements such as #weneeddiversebooks and #ownvoices. Ultimately, though, we argue that representation alone is not enough; White readers sometimes misunderstand texts that represent racial perspectives that are different from our own. In these cases, English teachers need tools for helping students read differently. To those ends, we propose racialized reader response for engaging White readers in reflecting on the ways Whiteness influences personal responses to texts.

COMMON CHALLENGE:
WHITE READERS' MISREADINGS OF BLACKNESS IN LITERATURE

Recently, in one of Carlin's courses, students read *The Crossover* by Kwame Alexander. *The Crossover* features the voice of Josh, a talented basketball player on the same team as his twin brother with whom he shares his love of the sport. They are supported by their former professional ball-playing father, and their mother, who is also the assistant principal at their school. The novel features a close-knit, Black family whose central conflict is the loving relationship between twin brothers as they also worry over their father's health. Carlin selected the novel for several reasons: She wanted to familiarize her students with the work of Kwame Alexander, an award-winning Black poet and young adult author; the book itself earned both a Newbery and a Coretta Scott King Award; and this verse novel, with a structure that mirrors a basketball game, is a highly engaging story that represents a Black family in positive and empowering ways. They read the book together with an article considering features of African American literature in children's and young adult literature (e.g., references to spirituality, church culture, and folklore; references to musical and oral traditions; nonlinear storytelling structure; use of African American English and language play; content based on the African American experience and reflective of political empowerment) (e.g., Henderson, 2005). Pertinent to this anecdote: Alexander does not label the characters as Black in the book.

Carlin's students opened the whole-class discussion by talking about the many things they really loved in the text: themes of family and sibling relationships, the playful language and fast-moving plot, the focus on basketball and Alexander's creative use of aspects of the game in the structure of the text, and the positive life lessons that all readers can take away from the book. At some point in the discussion, noticing that no one had mentioned race as it related to the story, especially given this course's explicit focus on racial and cultural diversity in children's and young adult literature, Carlin turned their attention to evidence of African American literary traditions in the text. Several students, all of whom identified as White, noted that the book did not "seem Black." In fact, several students said that they did not realize that the characters were African American until Carlin asked this question. In response, Carlin pointed to several indicators of African American identity and culture: the main character's use of African American vernacular; the main character's dreadlocks; references to several African American jazz and hip-hop artists throughout; a familiar, racially charged scene where Josh's father is pulled over by a White police officer; the conversation Josh's mother has with him about how to respond if he ever finds himself in an encounter with a police officer himself; the racial identity of the author; and even an illustration of the main character—albeit a shadowy silhouette—on the cover of the book. Students continued to question the racial identity of the main character, even as they discussed these aspects of the text. One White female student wondered whether assuming that the main characters were African American based on their use of African American vernacular, for example, constituted stereotyping. Another White male student noted, "It is a book about a Black kid, but it isn't a book about racism."

WHY THIS MATTERS FROM AN ANTIRACIST PERSPECTIVE

This example of the ways White students interpreted a story about contemporary Black characters is fruitful for thinking about the ways teachers' text selections influence students' thinking about race and racism, as well as the ways Whiteness shapes students' reading of those texts.

Whiteness as Default

At first, Carlin felt a little surprised that students did not immediately recognize the main characters in this story as Black. Her first response was to locate the misunderstanding in students' lack of familiarity with African American culture and identity. And maybe they had not read the assigned article? Upon further reflection, however, Carlin realized that these responses were not unique; rather, they were indicative of the way White readers often respond to texts featuring characters of color.

In many ways, this situation resembled the social media uproar that occurred in response to the casting of Rue of *The Hunger Games* film as Black (see Garcia & Haddix, 2014). In the novel, Collins describes Rue as "a twelve-year-old girl from District 11. She has dark brown skin and eyes, but other than that, she's very like Prim in size and demeanor" (p. 45). Despite this description, many White readers, surprised and upset when a Black actress was cast to play Rue in the movie, responded with racist social media posts and tweets. On this topic, Garcia and Haddix argue, "Because of the prevalence of White, hegemonic characters in texts like Collins' (2008) *The Hunger Games,* it is *literally* unimaginable for some readers to see depictions of characters other than White. That the text dictates characters like Rue and Thresh as non-White in the book does little to change the hegemonic climate in which many people read" (p. 213, emphasis in original). We understand this "hegemonic climate" to include the dominant White racial ideology that operates through both readers and texts. In other words, because literature has been dominated by Whiteness, readers assume that characters are White unless they are explicitly named as otherwise; and White readers steeped in a dominant White racial ideology bring their own assumptions and expectations to texts (e.g., McCormick, 1994). White readers are so used to assuming Whiteness in the characters they read about that they not only assume Whiteness, but they often, as was the case with Rue, resist when their assumptions turn out to be inaccurate.

We see parallels in the example we present in this chapter. Whiteness operated as such a powerful default that Carlin's students continued to question the possibility that the main character was Black, despite evidence to the contrary in the text.

Dominance of Whiteness in Literature Curriculum

Garcia and Haddix's (2014) argument leads us to contextualize White readers' individual responses within the ways the typical literature curriculum reflects and constructs Whiteness as the dominant, default racial perspective. Research in the field of English education has shown that typical literature curriculum continues to be dominated by White voices in terms of both authors and characters in familiar texts such as *Romeo and Juliet, The Great Gatsby, Adventures of Huckleberry Finn,* and *To Kill a Mockingbird* (Applebee, 1993; Cooperative Children's Book Center, 2016; Stallworth et al., 2006). In fact, studies conducted over a span of more than a decade have documented that none of the most frequently taught texts feature main characters of color or were written by authors of color (see Table 3.1). This traditional literature curriculum, endorsed and institutionalized through schools, continues to position "literature" as White and to position White racial perspectives as central and neutral. Steeped in a literature curriculum dominated by Whiteness, White readers bring these previous literary experiences, these assumptions about literature, and their strategies for reading to their responses to all texts.

Assumed White Readers

Whiteness dominates not only in terms of authorship and representation of characters, but also in terms of the assumed audience. Morrison (1992) asserts:

> Until very recently, and regardless of the race of the author, the readers of virtually all of American fiction have been positioned as White. I am interested to know what that assumption has meant to the literary imagination. When does racial "unconsciousness" or awareness of race enrich interpretive language, and when does it impoverish it? What does positing one's writerly self, in the wholly racialized society that is the United States, as unraced and all others as raced entail? What happens to the writerly imagination of a black author who is at some level always conscious of representing one's own race to, or in spite of, a race of readers that understands itself to be "universal" or race-free? In other words, how is "literary whiteness" and "literary blackness" made, and what is the consequence of that construction? How do embedded assumptions of racial (and not racist) language work in the literary enterprise that hopes and sometimes claims to be "humanistic"? (p. xii)

What has assuming a White readership meant to the literary imagination? To answer Morrison's question, one thing this assumption has meant is that authors—Black and White—have often explicitly named Black characters as Black, while not explicitly naming White characters as White. The effect of this practice has been an emphasis on Black characters as "raced" and White characters as "race-free," as Morrison points out. Alexander's decision not to label characters as Black in this case makes this assumption visible. Without the typical cue of an explicit label, Carlin's students questioned how they could know that the main characters were Black.

In the context of a literature curriculum dominated by White racial ideology, Carlin's students' responses to *The Crossover* may be less surprising. Their responses make visible the influence of Whiteness as an ideology that White readers bring to texts. This analysis is meant to illustrate consequences of literature curriculum and instruction that overrepresent White perspectives, thereby teaching students lessons—whether we, as English teachers, intend these lessons or not—about Whiteness as the "normal" or default

Table 3.1. Commonly Taught Texts

Applebee (1993)	Stallworth et al. (2006)
1. *Romeo and Juliet* (1597) by William Shakespeare	1. *To Kill a Mockingbird* (1960) by Harper Lee
2. *Macbeth* (1623) by William Shakespeare	2. *The Great Gatsby* (1925) by F. Scott Fitzgerald
3. *Adventures of Huckleberry Finn* (1884) by Mark Twain	3. *The Scarlet Letter* (1850) by Nathaniel Hawthorne
4. *Julius Caesar* (1623) by William Shakespeare	4. *Romeo and Juliet* (1597) by William Shakespeare
5. *To Kill a Mockingbird* (1960) by Harper Lee	5. *Julius Caesar* (1623) by William Shakespeare
6. *The Scarlet Letter* (1850) by Nathaniel Hawthorne	6. *The Crucible* (1953) by Arthur Miller
7. *Of Mice and Men* (1937) by John Steinbeck	7. *Macbeth* (1623) by William Shakespeare
8. *Hamlet* (1603) by William Shakespeare	8. *Adventures of Huckleberry Finn* (1884) by Mark Twain
9. *The Great Gatsby* (1925) by F. Scott Fitzgerald	9. *Animal Farm* (1945) by George Orwell
10. *Lord of the Flies* (1954) by William Golding	10. *A Separate Peace* (1953) by John Knowles

racial perspective. It also emphasizes the importance of disrupting traditional literature curriculum with literature by and about people of color, including literature that positions White readers as outsiders in ways that challenge White racial ideology.

"Single Stories" of People of Color Focused on Racism

Carlin's students not only assumed Whiteness; they also operated with a "single story" (Adiche, 2009) of Black characters as one about racism. One student said, "It doesn't hit you over the head; it isn't a book about racism." Students went on to note how few of the works about people of color that they had encountered were focused *not* on racism, but instead on topics like close-knit families, dating, or wanting to succeed at a sport, for example.

Looking back, Carlin can see how text selections in the first weeks of this course may have set her students up to expect that stories about people of color would center the topic of racism. In the first weeks, the class explored the ways White supremacy has been written into American history.

Along with Spring's textbook *Deculturalization and the Struggle for Equality* (2016), they read a range of historical fiction and nonfiction, including *My Name Is Seepeetza* by Shirley Sterling, *Copper Sun* by Sharon Draper, *Weedflower* by Cynthia Kadohata, and *Esperanza Rising* by Pam Munoz Ryan. On the one hand, this first section of the course was immensely important, because many students had never learned about Native American boarding schools, as they did through *My Name Is Seepeetza*. Many of them said that their study of the Atlantic slave trade had been "Whitewashed" compared with the graphic representation of the cruelty of the slave trade in *Copper Sun*. Many students said that their learning about World War II had never included mention of the Japanese internment camps depicted in *Weedflower*. The history of racism in immigration and citizenship was also not a topic they had explored, as they did in *Esperanza Rising*. Reading this set of texts in combination helped students comprehend the ways racism has worked systematically in the United States through laws, language policy, schools, and citizenship.

On the other hand, it seemed these literature selections contributed to an emphasis on stories about people of color as stories of ra*cism*. The repetition of stories about people of color within narratives about racial oppression had set up this expectation. Perhaps because the first four novels recounted experiences with racism for people of color, students expected more of the same with *The Crossover*.

Typical secondary literature curriculum, too, contributes to this "single story" (Adiche, 2009). Note that on the rare occasion when characters of color appear in the list of most frequently taught texts in high school (see Table 3.1), those characters are depicted within narratives about racism in every case. Tom Robinson is killed because a racist jury found him guilty of assaulting a White woman. Jim is a slave. Even in texts in which characters of color are featured in secondary roles, such as Crooks in *Of Mice and Men*, they are depicted as the subject of racism.

Carlin's students' responses are not unique in this regard either; White readers' expectations of single stories of racism in texts featuring characters of color supersede what the texts actually depict. When Groenke and her co-authors (2015) wrote about how their White teacher candidates typically talk about the Black male character Steve Harmon, in Walter Dean Myers's *Monster*, they shared the ways White readers fail to notice how loving and supportive Steve's family is throughout the trial. Instead, White readers think of this narrative as "another" story about a Black kid falling through the cracks because he doesn't have a strong family foundation.

This analysis emphasizes the implications of a narrow, traditional literature curriculum, one that disproportionately represents characters of color in terms of their experiences with racism. It points to the importance of representing many, many stories of people of color in secondary and post-secondary literature selections (Thomas, 2019).

Emphasis on Historical Representations of People of Color

Importantly, starting the course with a look at the ways racism has operated historically in the United States set the stage for more complex understandings of the ways the legacy of that racism is still at work today. Students brought this historical understanding to texts they read later in the course. For example, students applied understanding about the lasting consequences of Native American boarding schools—for families, language, culture, identity—to their reading of a contemporary Native American character in *Absolutely True Diary of a Part-time Indian*, a novel by Sherman Alexie about Arnold or "Junior," a Native American boy who makes the decision to leave the reservation where he lives to attend the White-dominant school in a neighboring town.

Carlin's students also reflected on the fact that they had never before encountered a contemporary story about Native Americans in school; in middle and high school they had encountered Native Americans mostly as they were represented in history textbooks and historical literature. Continually representing racism as a thing of the past creates problems. First, it characterizes racism as a problem that is no longer relevant, or no longer as virulent as it once was. Focusing on historical stories of racism reinforces the misleading idea that the world has moved into a "post-racial society" that is over this problem. Second, when the English curriculum features only stories of people of color set in the past, it neglects to "see" people of color today.

For teachers as well as students, it may be easier to discuss racism as a thing of the past. Keeping the "problem" of racism in the past tense increases the chances that classroom talk will not explode with volatility, will not expose racial and experiential differences among students in the room. We will have more to say about race talk in Chapter 6.

Representation Is Not Enough

Following the discussion recounted above, Carlin and her students used a journal article about the Black Arts Movement (e.g., Henderson, 2005) to discuss features of African American literature in Alexander's *The Crossover*. They considered the influence of musical forms, especially jazz and hip-hop, not only through the storyline but also in the rhythm of Alexander's poetic style. They discussed the use of African American Vernacular English, especially word play and signifyin'. And, they debated whether the structure of the novel—organized into the four quarters of a basketball game, each characterized by varied but repeated poetic forms—constituted a nonlinear, episodic storytelling structure. Their collective analysis of these features of the text contributed to a greater understanding of *The Crossover* as not only a story about Black characters but also reflective of features of an African American storytelling style (e.g., Fox & Short, 2003; Glenn, 2014).

EFFECTS OF LITERATURE CURRICULUM ON STUDENTS OF COLOR

This book prioritizes teaching about race and racism in predominantly White contexts, and the opening example is meant to illustrate that White-dominant literature curriculum contributes to Whiteness operating as a default in literary responses of many White readers. But what are the experiences of students of color who are marginalized in a variety of ways in predominantly White schools? Baker-Bell et al. (2017), building on the work of Love (2017), characterize the omission of authors and characters of color in literature as one of the many examples of symbolic violence that students of color face in school. English teachers, they argue, must understand that choosing Eurocentric texts that omit the lived realities of Black people, or misrepresent the multiple ways of being Black, leads to anti-Blackness and the devaluation of Black life. They go on to say:

> We [English teachers] also invoke racial violence on Black and Brown youth when we don't include literature that portrays Black and Brown people as heroes and victors. We invoke racial violence when we fail to portray Black and Brown women as heroines and activists. (pp. 123–124)

Our literature selections communicate to students that they belong (or not), that they are valued (or not), that their identities and experiences are welcome in the classroom (or not). Literature curriculum that prioritizes White characters and White readers precludes students of color from seeing their identity reflected as part of the classroom community.

The dominance of White perspectives and the omission of people of color in the literature curriculum may influence the kind of experience students of color have not only with literature but also with reading. Allyn and Morrell (2016) note that so much about reading instruction begins with the ways that students are included in a reading community, the ways their identities are valued and validated, and their feelings of confidence and belonging in a reading community. Our literature selections can help or hinder students of color in this regard. The NCTE *Resolution on the Need for Diverse Children's and Young Adult Books* (2015a) points to the omission of diverse books in school curriculum as additional evidence of inequity in school curriculum and instruction.

Moreover, literature curriculum that tells exclusively a single story about people of color as *subjects of racism* also has detrimental effects on students of color. We join many others in worrying that, too often, stories in typical literature curriculum frame students of color only in terms of racism. In a recent interview, Thomas (2018) highlighted the effects of stories of Black pain for Black students:

EFFECTS OF LITERATURE CURRICULUM ON STUDENTS OF COLOR, CONTINUED

After a while, Black children begin to dislike just reading Black books. . . . I am having the hardest time getting the high school students to read a Black historical book. They even chose to read *The Handmaid's Tale* over Octavia Butler's *Kindred*. I think some of that is internalized White supremacy and anti-Blackness. But some of it is just fatigue around Black pain, specifically for Black children. . . . Kids need a balance of stories, although we don't have many stories that are not about Black pain. . . . The books about slavery, gang members, or somebody on drugs—there's really no relief from those kinds of narratives, while other kinds of literature are riven with stereotypes.

What does it mean for Black children that, when Blackness is represented in the curriculum at all, it is only through difficult stories? Students of color may internalize stereotypical images. All children in schools deserve to have their identities reflected in ways that are not always sad, depressing, or painful. Students of color deserve a wide range of stories that are uplifting—without having to focus exclusively on civil rights or other historical heroes. They deserve stories that explore a wide range of genres and topics, including family stories about parents, siblings, and falling in love, for example.

Although Carlin and her students discussed the main characters' Blackness and features of African American literature, what they did not discuss was readers' Whiteness. Whiteness and White racial identity were topics of much discussion in the course, but in this particular instance, the failure to discuss White readers' colorblind interpretation of the text stands out as glaringly obvious. Garcia and Haddix (2014) argue:

The teacher education classroom must operate as a space where beginning and practicing teachers can openly dialogue about underlying assumptions and colorblind ideologies that they too have when engaging with texts like *The Hunger Games* (Collins, 2008). When readers say that they do not see race when reading young adult literature, they are perpetuating a whiteness by default standpoint. (p. 214)

In this scenario, Carlin could have taken the discussion a step further, asking students to reflect on the ways their own White racial identities contributed to their reading of the characters as White. In the next section, we propose a racialized reader response designed to capitalize on this possibility.

WHAT YOU CAN DO:
INTERRUPT WHITENESS VIA TEXT SELECTION
AND LITERARY RESPONSE

The opening example emphasizes the need to populate our literature curriculum with myriad stories representing people of color—including of happy, successful lives—across grade levels, over time, and within a course. It also suggests, however, that representation alone is not enough. As English teachers, we must engage White readers with those representations in ways that expose Whiteness, interrupt stereotypes, and offer students alternative grounds on which to base their interpretations. In this section, we lay out principles to guide text selection and to racialize readers' responses to literature.

Before we lay out principles, however, we would like to acknowledge that, as English teachers, we often do not have total freedom to change course texts; changes to literature curriculum frequently are made at a department or district level. Even when individual teachers are involved in those curricular decisions, often they are made in collaboration with others who may have competing pedagogical goals. Whether teachers have the freedom to select texts on their own or are working in collaboration with grade-level, department-level, or district-level teams to revise curriculum, the principles below may be useful for identifying gaps and prioritizing changes.

We suggest beginning by making a list of all texts included in existing literature curriculum, including book-length works, short stories, poems, informational texts, and multimedia texts. Depending on whether teachers are collaborating with colleagues or working on their own, they could consider approaching this activity by looking across grade levels, within a department, or within one course. Looking at a complete list of texts, teachers can use the sets of questions in the sections below to think about whether and how race and racism are represented across the literature curriculum.

Principle 1: Prioritize Book-Length Works by and About People of Color

Foregrounding voices of people of color in literature curriculum is a top priority. The #weneeddiversebooks campaign argues that all children deserve mirrors, windows, and sliding doors to represent their complex and multilayered identities (Bishop, 1990). You might begin by identifying:

- Which titles in my literature curriculum feature characters of color? What roles do those characters play in the story? Are those characters in primary or secondary roles? How are those characters portrayed?
- Do these texts represent a variety of racial and cultural identities?

Moreover, the #ownvoices campaign recognizes that interrupting the dominance of White voices in literature must go beyond representation of characters of color to also foreground literature authored by people who share the identities of the characters they are writing about. Although the publishing industry is still working to make the diversity represented in children's and young adult literature reflect the diversity of the United States, English teachers have many rich and engaging texts by and about people of color to choose from. As you examine your list, you might consider:

- By whom have these texts been written?
- Are authors of color equally represented?
- Are stories about characters of color written by authors who share those identities?
- Are stories about racism authored by people who share the racial identity featured in the stories?

It is also important to ensure that your curriculum includes stories by and about people of color centrally and not only as texts complementing the main literary fare written by and featuring White characters. In other words, book-length works carry weight in the curriculum. Book-length works—versus short stories, poems, and supplementary texts—communicate something about which voices are positioned as important. So, as you examine your existing titles, you might consider:

- Which book-length titles in my literature curriculum are written by people of color?
- Are authors and characters of color represented in book-length works? Or are they "supplemented in" through short stories, poems, and other shorter works?

A few texts to consider include: *Narrative of the Life of Frederick Douglass*; *The Bluest Eye*; *Their Eyes Were Watching God*; *Copper Sun*; *March*; and *Monster*. Of course, these are only a few of the many options you might consider. We selected just a few examples to illustrate the kinds of texts that have the potential to position White readers as outsiders, to expose a limited White worldview. They also provide a platform for accompanying conversations that have the potential to shine a light on and interrupt the ways Whiteness operates through an assumed worldview.

Principle 2: Include Myriad Contemporary and Empowering Stories About People of Color

Our aim is to overcome the "single stories" (Adiche, 2009) of people of color as stories about racism to also tell contemporary, empowering, and positive stories. To move toward telling a multitude of rich, complex stories that represent racial identity intersecting with other identity markers—age, class, sexuality, language, geography, religion, and ability. Here, we invite you to examine your list, to ask:

- In what years were texts by and about people of color written? What eras do they portray? Does the literature curriculum include contemporary representations of people of color?
- Does my literature curriculum include stories that represent people of color in a variety of ways, including in empowering, celebratory, positive stories? Which texts include positive representations of people of color? Which texts explore the topic of racism exclusively?
- Does my literature curriculum represent a range of stories of people of color in which race intersects with other aspects of diversity, including gender, class, geography, sexual orientation, ability, and religion?

Teachers also may think about this point by considering the perspectives they represent when they explore particular themes or genres in literature. For example, Thomas (2018, 2019) discusses the need to disrupt the single story of urban youth as one that characterizes people of color as poor and dangerous, reinforcing the "single story" of what urban settings mean and attaching it to Brown and Black communities. She advocates for more stories in urban settings that feature White poverty and Black middle-class families, for example. Similarly, Toliver (2018) found that many of the mirror texts often selected for Black girls represent "single stories" of Black girls as living in the northeast, from urban backgrounds, and dealing with teen pregnancy, violence, and abuse. Toliver encourages teachers to look beyond the typical publishing houses and award winners to find science fiction and fantasy novels that represent Black girls in a variety of ways through a variety of genres.

Recently, enthusiastic momentum has been building around Afrofuturist texts. Difficult to define, Afrofuturist texts blend elements of science fiction, historical fiction, speculative fiction, fantasy, Afrocentricity, and magic realism with non-Western beliefs. In some cases, it is a total reenvisioning of the past and speculation about the future rife with cultural critiques (Womack, 2013, cited in Kaplan & Garcia, 2019). In the aptly titled *How Long 'Til Black Future Month?* (2018), Afrofuturist author N.K. Jemisin explains her love of science fiction and fantasy. As a young Black female reader, she craved being able to see herself in the futures imagined in such texts. Teachers might embed Afrofuturist texts into their curriculum as a way to offer all students visions of a future that centralize Blackness, a criticality of our racist past and present, and fantastic imaginings.

Butler (2017) calls attention to how rarely texts by Black women authors, especially nonfiction texts such as memoirs and autobiographies, are taught. This absence of Black women's autobiographies and memoirs, she argues, "is indicative of a larger form of historical amnesia" (p. 156). English teachers can call attention to the lives and social activism of Black women by prioritizing their autobiographies and memoirs.

The following are a few selections that might help teachers consider how to complicate representations of Blackness with stories that are contemporary, of a range of genres, and also positive: *Assata: The Autobiography of Assata Shakur*; *Americanah*; "Recitatif"; *Children of Blood and Bone*; *Akata Witch*; *The Poet X*; and *One Crazy Summer*.

When considering representations of Blackness in their literature curriculum, English teachers might ask: When students read about great, supportive, loving families, are those families also Black? Can depictions of school experiences centering Black boys be positive? What do representations of love and dating look like involving Black youth? When a novel foregrounds family problems, could those be about worrying about a loving Black parent's health, for example? What if class worries about survival didn't always involve Black people in school-read stories?

Principle 3: Ensure That the Curriculum Reflects Texts by and About People of Color Across the Year

So often, when English teachers turn to texts by and about people of color, those texts occupy a literary corner of the curriculum in an additive fashion (Banks, 2001), and that ends the treatment of "that group" for the year. The temporal positioning of texts speaks volumes to students "studying" the ways value is signaled by text length, curriculum order, and timing. For literary curriculum to have an impact on racial literacy learning for all students, but especially White students who otherwise may not have extensive contact with people of color in segregated communities, teachers can ensure that literature by and about people of color populates the curriculum across the year (Skerrett, 2011). As teachers look at their lists, they might ask:

- Are texts by authors of color, featuring characters of color, represented across the curriculum, rather than clustered in "multicultural" themes?
- How might texts by and about people of color more densely populate the curriculum?
- How might reordering the placement of texts by and about people of color reflect the school's prioritizing of such stories and racial ideologies?

Principle 4: Racialize White Readers' Responses to Literature

The opening scenario suggests that representation through text selection may not be enough to interrupt Whiteness as a default when White readers encounter literature that reflects racial experiences that are different from our own. White readers also need instruction for uncovering ways Whiteness operates ideologically to shape our responses to literature. Here, we propose a racialized reader response as an approach for making visible for White readers the ways Whiteness shapes our responses to texts.

English teachers familiar with traditional reader response know that the approach generally acknowledges that readers make meaning through their transactions with texts and that the meaning they make depends as much on what the readers bring to their reading of the text—personal experiences, literary experiences, values, assumptions, purposes for reading, to name a few—as it does on the text itself (e.g., Beach, 1993; Rosenblatt, 1995). Critics of reader response have noted, however, that reader response may be limiting when White readers encounter books that represent racial and cultural experiences that differ from our own (e.g., Lewis, 2000; Rabinowitz & Smith, 1998). In other words, readers, especially White readers, often identify with such texts, focusing on universal themes and personal connections in ways that gloss over or distort racial and cultural difference (Dressel, 2005; Glazier & Seo, 2005; Rabinowitz & Smith, 1997). In response, critics have suggested that reader response should help readers consider the ways responses are shaped ideologically (e.g., Lewis, 2000; McCormick, 1994).

To compensate for these common limitations, we have adapted traditional reader response questions to help White readers racialize responses to literature. To illustrate, classic reader response asks readers to consider the question: How does the text, who I am, and the context in which I am reading this text right now affect my interpretations of the text? Racialized reader response asks readers to consider: How does my racial identity and the racial discourse that dominates for me, together with the text and context that I am reading through right now, affect my literary interpretations? In Table 3.2, we have adapted Appleman's (2015) reader response chart, a configuration of context, text, and reader, to organize ideas about what kinds of questions, analyses, and examples make productive racialized reader responses possible.

Racialized reader response aims to help White readers understand that Whiteness operates not only as a racial category but also as a racial ideology that organizes the way people see the world. It aims to make readers aware of the ways texts, as well as their responses to texts, are shaped by this racial ideology. And, it is intended to challenge the invisibility of Whiteness by making the influence of Whiteness more visible to readers and by including discussions of Whiteness as part of business as usual in literature study.

Table 3.2. Racialized Reader Response

Context

- What is the racial context in which you are reading this text—either in terms of social climate or the classroom context? What social issues or current events are pertinent? What are the racial dynamics of your classroom environment?

- What are your purposes for reading this text? How do those purposes inform your experience with this text? How is a critical race analysis relevant to your purposes?

Text	Reader
• What are major plot points? In what ways does the plot reinforce or interrupt dominant or stereotypical ways of thinking about race or racism?	• What is your racial identity? How does your racial identity shape your reading of this text?
• What are major themes? In what ways do the themes reinforce or interrupt dominant ways of thinking about race or racism?	• Does the text position you as a racial insider or an outsider? How do you know? How does this positioning influence your reading experience?
• How are characters developed? Are characters of color round and dynamic or flat and static? What roles do characters of color play in the plot? Are characters represented in stereotypical ways?	• What are aspects of the text to which you can relate? How might *not* relating to a character in a novel in terms of race or power be important for you as a reader—or important for learning about your racial identity?
• How does the form or style of the book reflect the racial perspective of the text (or not)?	• Are there aspects of the text that you find unfamiliar, uncertain, or challenging? What might those aspects reveal to you about your own racial assumptions and perspectives?
• What is the racial identity of the author? How does the author's racial or cultural background contribute to or take away from the text's authenticity?	• Are there aspects of the text that cause feelings of discomfort, uncertainty, or resistance? What might these aspects of the text reveal to you about your own experiences or assumptions?
• What is the racial identity of the intended audience of this text? How do you know?	

Racialized reader response helps White readers consider how our assumptions may constrain or distort our understanding of a text, as it did in the opening scenario. In fact, McCormick (1994) suggests that these moments of "mismatch" have great potential for making visible the values, beliefs, and assumptions readers bring to a text. Knowing this, a racialized reader response is designed to capitalize on moments of tension, mismatch, uncertainty, and discomfort. English teachers might help students embrace these moments as opportunities for potential growth.

IN THE CLASSROOM: RACIALIZING WHITE READERS' RESPONSES TO *THE CROSSOVER*

Although Carlin did not use racialized reader response in her class at the time, here we imagine how she might have used it to deepen her students' collective analysis. Using the questions in Table 3.2 as a guide, Carlin and her students might have explored issues specific to their reading of *The Crossover*, such as:

Reader. *The Crossover* is a book by a Black author and about Black characters. Several White students in the class mistook the characters for White or were reluctant to assume Black identities despite features of the text. Knowing that moments of mismatch like these can help to make racial assumptions visible, Carlin might have asked her students to consider: What does this misreading help us understand about our own racial identities, the racial dynamics of this class, or the dominant racial ideology of our society? What are consequences of such a misreading?

Text. It is common in literature for White characters not to be labeled racially, while characters of color often are. Alexander made a deliberate decision not to label the main characters as Black. Carlin might have called greater attention to this particular detail by asking students: Why do you think he made this choice? What does this decision contribute to themes of the text? What are consequences of this choice for you as a reader? What does assuming Whiteness reveal to you about the racial assumptions we made as a class?

Or, Carlin and her students might have noted that Alexander depicted a reality of police brutality toward Blacks in at least two scenes. Together, Carlin and her students might have explored: How do your own racialized and politicized beliefs about police brutality with regard to Black people affect how you read those scenes?

Context. Carlin might have called attention to the way that context shaped the reading of the text by commenting: We are reading this text

SAMPLE UNIT PLAN FOR *THE CROSSOVER*

After reading about how *The Crossover* was interpreted as "White" by Carlin's students, a preservice teacher in Sophia's class, Julianna Campbell, designed the unit described here. Her objectives were to help White students recognize racial cues and understand the impact of race in their interpretation. Specifically, Julianna wanted middle school students to be able to identify explicit and implicit messages regarding race in the novel. She utilizes the image and metaphor of an iceberg to convey the difference between what you see about an iceberg as *explicit*, and the so-much that remains underwater that parallels *implicit* messages in texts. To drive home this teaching, she guides students to Alexander's poem "Ode to My Hair," (p. 33) where the protagonist lauds the beauty of his dreadlocks. She prompts students to consider, What does the poem say explicitly about his hair? She guides them to see his hair compared to a tree, treated like gold, the amount of care he directs to it before a game, and his decline of a bet tied to having to cut his hair, because it is so important to him.

Next, Julianna teaches students about the poetic form of an ode. She instructs how it celebrates an important person, place, or thing; that it has Ancient Greek origins; and that White, Romantic poets popularized it. Her next question shifts the focus to implicit messages in literature: Why might Alexander have used *this* form? What implicit messages is he sharing with this choice? Now she directs students to notice how the protagonist exaggerates his love of his hair, but also how Alexander reinvents a White poetic form by using it to direct attention to racial identifiers tied to the body (e.g., hair). To ensure that this claim about how Alexander is using form to draw attention to race and racism, Julianna includes direct instruction on the historical objectification of the Black body. By sharing images in a presentation (e.g., of lynching, of racist caricatures), Julianna asks students to consider, How is the Black body treated in history? And then, What might Alexander's "Ode to My Hair" be commenting on by praising Black hair, and, by extension, Black bodies, through a White literary form? After leading them through this close reading of the text, but also of historical images of the Black body, Julianna closes her lesson by asking students, How does an examination of Alexander's use of form expose explicit and implicit representations of race?

within the context of a teacher preparation course that highlights standards that ask teacher candidates to "plan and implement English language arts and literacy instruction that promotes social justice and critical engagement with complex issues related to maintaining a diverse, inclusive, equitable society" (NCTE, 2012). She might have asked: How does this context affect the ways you read this novel?

Carlin's initial approach of asking students to explore characteristics of African American literature in *The Crossover* may have engaged her students productively with racial difference by helping them recognize and appreciate the influence of African American literary traditions in the text. For this reason, we do not suggest that racialized reader response would replace that approach. Rather, we see these approaches as being complementary, working to make visible different aspects of racial understanding. In other words, we see racialized reader response as an additional tool English teachers can use in concert with other approaches to deepen students' experiences with texts.

CONCLUSION

Exploring Whiteness can be difficult with White students. The process of learning to see Whiteness, of questioning deeply held assumptions and beliefs, can be emotional, uncertain, and stressful. So, how can we encourage White readers to take this risk? While we do not suggest that this work is easy, we have found that discussing the ways Whiteness as an ideology works on us all can be productive for opening students up to this work. Even if we begin there, White students sometimes get stuck in shame or guilt in their early explorations of Whiteness. It is possible to help them move past this paralysis to see how becoming aware of Whiteness, and questioning how it works, is part of the process toward critical awareness and social change. We explore White racial identity work in much more detail in Chapter 7.

CHAPTER 4

Unearthing Whiteness in Canonical Texts About Racism

> I am grateful that among the many indignities inflicted on me in childhood, I escaped *Huckleberry Finn*.
>
> —Julius Lester, *To Be a Slave*

In the previous chapter, we explored the issue of text selection in the context of antiracist literature instruction. In this chapter, we turn to the other side of the same coin—toward treatment of canonical works by White authors on the topic of racism. This chapter confronts challenges and opportunities that come with teaching texts like *To Kill a Mockingbird* and *Adventures of Huckleberry Finn*, with an in-depth focus on the latter in this chapter. While the previous chapter centered on text selection through the concept of *different reading*, this chapter focuses on what to do if one must or one chooses to teach canonical texts through *reading differently* (Morrell, 2018).

COMMON CHALLENGE: WHITE INVESTMENTS IN CANONICAL WHITE SAVIOR NARRATIVES

Sophia has a framed poster in her living room of Mark Twain performing at the Brooklyn Academy of Music, a sign of how much she has revered Twain's humor, and, yes, his treatment of racism, for decades. This love of Twain and *Huckleberry Finn* began during her junior year of high school, when she learned this adulation from her English teacher, who inspired her to teach English herself. Via setting analysis, this teacher traced the increase in human cruelty as Huck and Jim descended further south on the Mississippi. She helped students notice the humor of Twain's satire in the novel through Huck's colorful phrasings. And Sophia's teacher emphasized the poignancy of Huck's decision to help Jim even if he believed that it meant going to hell. Sophia remembers feeling so good "participating" as a reader in Huck's decision to help Jim, joining other readers of this canonical text who understood the importance of the scene.

WHY THIS MATTERS FROM AN ANTIRACIST PERSPECTIVE

Representations of Whiteness

When English teachers focus on race or racism in literature, we usually focus our analysis on portrayals of people of color. According to Julius Lester (1984/2004) and other critics like Toni Morrison, however, the lessons we are teaching "about" racism, through these White-authored, canonical text selections, say more about Whiteness than about Blackness. With regard to *Huckleberry Finn* specifically, Morrison (1992) argues that Twain, like other White, canonical authors, establishes a clear portrait of Whiteness in the book far more than one of Blackness.

> It is not what Jim seems that warrants inquiry, but what Mark Twain, Huck, and especially Tom need from him that should solicit our attention. In that sense the book may indeed be "great" because in its structure, in the hell it puts its readers through at the end, the frontal debate it forces, it simulates and describes the parasitical nature of white freedom. (p. 57)

Morrison defines the "greatness" of this novel in ways opposite from those upholding the book's merits. She sees the novel as an accurate reflection of a racist U.S. history and present that perennially delays a promised freedom to Blacks, and instead continues to require Blacks' inferiority in order for Whites to continue to be "free." The endlessly deferred end of the novel, because of Tom Sawyer's antics, mirrors the sociocultural reality of Black people today: Like Jim, Black people in the United States are continuously promised a freer future, yet that promise never materializes. Morrison's critique of this canonical text exposes the ways White readers want to see themselves, and how they fail to see how such texts depict Black people in relation to Whites.

In fact, a key trait featured across the most commonly taught texts about racism is protagonists who function as White savior characters. As we will discuss again in Chapter 5 through strategies for *To Kill a Mockingbird*, characters like Huck and Atticus typically are interpreted as heroes precisely because of their actions on behalf of Black characters and on the side of racial equity. As an example, Huck typically is seen as heroic, especially because of his much-noted decision to help Jim escape slavery even if it means going to hell himself. Yet many readers are not impressed with what such "heroism" applauds. Jane Smiley (1996/2004), a White author, reminds us that Huck was prepared to go to hell well before this oft-cited moment in the novel, as a way to distinguish himself from the constraining Miss Watson. Once he heard that she intended to go to "the good place," he decided he, "couldn't see no advantage in going where she was going." This reminder releases some of the air from the more racially heroic scene about his willingness to go to hell for Jim.

Our opening anecdote features Sophia's enduring love of this novel, especially the "heroic" scene around Huck's decision to save Jim. Why is this untempered love of the novel a problem? It fails to notice a reliance on a White savior character like Huck. It also neglects the fact that it's a story about racism by a White person about White people and for White people, a story that makes Whites look—and feel—good about our racial selves. Which means that a central problem with White savior stories is the limited way they portray Blackness: Black characters are in the story to prop up Whiteness, rather than as fully formed or complex characters.

Representations of Blackness

Let's look at the plot. Grateful for Huck's company, Jim follows him on the river, continuing even after they have turned away from the possibility of his freedom when they miss Cairo and drift further south. Black author and professor Julius Lester (1984/2004), who read the book as an adult for the first time, commented on this plot choice:

> If the reader must suspend intelligence to accept this, intelligence has to be dispensed with altogether to believe that Jim, having unknowingly passed the confluence of the Ohio and Mississippi Rivers, would continue down the river and go deeper and deeper into the heart of slave country. A century of white readers have accepted this as credible, a grim reminder of the abysmal feelings of superiority with which whites are burdened. (p. 366)

Lester emphasizes the extent to which surrendering to Twain's narrative arc could be seen as White readers succumbing to the portrayal of a Black adult as *understandably* ignorant and trusting of a White young boy who still believes in the rightness of slavery. For Lester and other Black readers, such credulity on the part of White readers matches the implicit racial hierarchies within U.S. society that are reinforced in literature.

Lester also pursues another side of Jim's portrayal in his critique, one featuring Jim's willing passivity toward Whites. In the scene late in the novel where Tom Sawyer has been shot and needs medical attention, the doctor attempting to treat Tom tells the story of how helpful Jim was to him and how easily Jim permitted the authorities to shackle him again:

> This depiction of a black "hero" is familiar by now since it has been repeated in countless novels and films. It is a picture of the only kind of black that whites have ever truly liked—faithful, tending sick whites, not speaking, not causing trouble, and totally passive. He is the archetypal "good nigger," who lacks self-respect, dignity, and a sense of self separate from the one whites want him to have. A century of white readers have accepted this characterization because it permits their own "humanity" to shine with more luster. (p. 367)

Lester's comments help us, the White authors, think about why it is that the U.S. literary curriculum might hold especially tight to *specific* portrayals of Blackness in the texts we choose, especially portrayals in books described by White teachers as helpful in teaching about racism. And, as we discussed in Chapter 3, when such depictions of Blackness prevail in the White literature curriculum in schools, it is no wonder that more complex, positive, and encouraging portrayals of Blackness in texts are not seen by White readers.

As a White reader and deep admirer of *Huckleberry Finn*, Sophia admits to not having realized previously how problematic Jim's portrayal as a Black man is. This realization alone is difficult to acknowledge as an author of this book and a teacher. At stake in neglecting or missing this key facet of text selection is the possibility—or likelihood—that the texts teachers use for *antiracist* aims work to *reinforce* problematic representations of Blackness. Admittedly, and as we will discuss below, not all readers—nor all Black readers—agree about how Twain portrays Blackness in this novel. For this reason, and as we will argue next, *how* teachers instruct this and other texts focused on racism matters greatly.

Use of Satiric Mode for Addressing Racism

For many readers and scholars who uphold *Huckleberry Finn*'s place in the canon, the key to this argument relies on unpacking Twain's use of satire to deliver his social critique. For example, African American scholar Jocelyn Chadwick-Joshua (1998) insists on Twain's consistent and estimable critique of racism in this text. For her, Jim—not Huck—is the hero. Her compelling interpretation shows Jim as the *active* agent in pursuing his own freedom, a character engendering the help of a White southern boy whose trust and respect he achieves through complex logomachies—verbal battles—in scenes like the King Solomon debate, which slowly convince this boy to fundamentally work against societal views he *believes in* about slavery. Key to Chadwick-Joshua's interpretation—and our own later in this chapter—is an enormously nuanced and complex understanding of the way satire works. Such an understanding opens up her reading of the text as one that emphasizes Twain's efforts toward verisimilitude, and his recognition that the deferment of Jim's freedom at the end imitates Twain's recognition of the limitations of post–Civil War freedom in the wake of Jim Crow.

What happens if students do not share this sophisticated understanding of satire? What if students miss or misunderstand Twain's use of satire in the novel? To make this point about the vulnerabilities around satire clear, White literary critic Jonathan Arac (1997/2004) turned to audience responses to a satirized television character from the 1970s: openly racist Archie Bunker of *All in the Family*. A very popular show of its time, *All in the Family* earned its popularity because it appealed to liberal viewers aware of its race critique *as well as* to conservative viewers who appreciated the character of Archie because he articulated what many Whites were thinking. Arac connects this problem to that of reading *Huckleberry Finn* in schools: "Twain and Lear [the show's producer] alike provoke different responses from different readers. It is offensive for cultural authorities to grant legitimacy to only a single way of reading" (p. 451). For some critics, this vulnerability of the text to racist interpretation suffices to make them want it out of the curriculum.

In short, when teachers' text choices for addressing racism rely on the satiric mode, a mode that challenges readers to follow twists and turns of meanings that are layered and complex, we risk students missing the *impact* of the social critique rendered through this mode. After all, when we present ideas like these to teachers in the field, their main concern is that often it is difficult for students just to stay with the dialect, the structure, the historical setting, and the length of this novel. It would not be far-fetched that the social critique rendered through satire might be lost or misunderstood completely, with this text *reinforcing* rather than *challenging* racism, if teachers are not careful.

Relationship Between Race and Canonicity

Of course, Sophia's experience is not unique. Many, many English teachers and their students have read this novel similarly over the years, reaffirming *Huckleberry Finn*'s place in the secondary literature canon. There are several effects of such literary canonicity. First, readers might ignore the active work it takes for a text to enter and remain an important enough piece of literature to be considered canonical. Texts are not self-evidently canonical; individuals, groups, and societies must agree, often for a range of reasons that may not include solely literary merit, that a text belongs in the canon (Kolbas, 2018). And such agreement may—and often does—shift over time to eject books once considered great. That said, once a novel has taken its place in the secondary literary canon, a host of institutional factors—from material resources, to the availability of pedagogical resources, to standards documents like the Common Core State Standards, to teachers' preferences and perceptions about what students "should" read—can prevent shifts in literary status from being reflected in schools' literature curricula.

Second, even if a text is considered canonical, that does not mean that it is unflawed or unproblematic. As African American literature professor Robert O'Meally discussed in his introduction to the novel, *Huckleberry Finn* has been considered an "unassailable monument . . . swallowed whole as a perfect book" (Twain, 1884/2003, p. xviii). We agree with O'Meally that there are no unassailable literary monuments. Students must understand this point as well so that texts are not treated with kid gloves, especially when those texts present offensive views of the students required to read them. Too often, when teachers rely on the argument of canonicity for a text's inclusion in the curriculum, the curriculum becomes a literary accolade parade, making critiques of author or text far more difficult. When teachers pick up such canonical texts without considering their place in anti-racist work, the status quo of centuries of racism gets reinforced.

Finally, as English teachers, we must consider the relationship between canonicity and novels about racism in particular. Looking at the lists we shared about commonly taught novels that focus on racism (see Table 3.1), we reiterate that in typical secondary literature curriculum, the topic of racism often is treated from a White-authored perspective—that of Mark Twain or Harper Lee, most notably. In fact, in a survey of English teachers in Michigan, Carlin found that when teachers addressed the topic of racism through literature, they reported doing so most often through commonly taught canonical texts written by White authors (Borsheim-Black, 2012). Moreover, in explaining their inclusion of these texts, teachers cited their commitment to teaching lessons about the history and present-day legacy of racism in the United States.

We do not question these teachers' desire to teach about race and racism. Rather, we wonder why it is that *these* are the novels about racism that get taught the most. Why do schools prioritize White voices on this topic? What do these novels afford the majority-White teachers who reach for them as texts that address racism? Regarding *Huckleberry Finn* specifically, we join other critics in arguing that this text's ironclad position in the English curriculum may be in part because it makes White readers feel good about our role in harmonious race relations in this country. Earlier in this chapter, Sophia shared feeling as though she, too, "participated" in making Huck's noble decision to help Jim escape, when she read this scene as a high school student. Such a feeling might be what wed her to this novel, to Twain, to Huck, to her teacher, ensuring that such feelings would get reproduced across generations of students through her own teaching of this novel.

WHAT YOU CAN DO:
EXPOSE WHITENESS IN CANONICAL, WHITE-AUTHORED TEXTS

To address the complexities of teaching White-authored, canonical texts focused on racism, we recommend four strategies.

Principle 1: Expose Whiteness

Rather than focus only on representations of *Blackness* in canonical literary selections, teachers can guide students to see how commonly taught texts about racism feature *Whiteness*. Whites are "colored" as much as any other racial group, and our racial portraits in literature work together to craft an

THE N-WORD

White teachers also might consider how a text like *Huckleberry Finn* might be experienced by students of color in White-dominant settings as yet another set of school-based racial microaggressions. We share remarks by Black readers about the effects of being *required* to hear the N-word read aloud in school. In an oft-cited letter published in the *New York Times* in 1982, Allan B. Ballard shares his experience as a Black student in a White-dominant school in the 1950s.

> I can still recall the anger I felt as my white classmates read aloud the word "nigger." In fact, as I write this letter I am getting angry all over again. I wanted to sink into my seat. Some of the whites snickered, others giggled. I can recall nothing of the literary merits of this work that you [*New York Times* author] term "the greatest of all American novels." I only recall the sense of relief I felt when I would flip ahead a few pages and see that the word "nigger" would not be read that hour. (cited in Henry, 1992/2004, pp. 386–387)

How many teachers, especially White teachers, have considered that reading this book aloud as a class, repeating language used to vilify Black people, might have the kinds of effects described by Ballard? Despite such complaints by many Black parents for decades, when challenges to the novel are made, teachers and schools hail the novel as a literary classic and claim that this justifies its place in the curriculum. Arac (2004) asks:

> How great must artists be before we trust them so much that their words are treated not only as unchangeable but also as obligatory? How much must a slur hurt, and whom, before we decide that it need not be made a compulsory part of what Cochran called the everyday "offensive treatment" that mars the ongoing racial life of the United States? (p. 449)

We address the reading of the N-word in a teaching context specifically in Chapter 6. Here, we affirm that we do not support censorship or book banning in general. However, when a text proves so offensive to students *required* to read it and have it read *aloud*, in *mandatory, public* schooling, especially a term garnering such rage and humiliation for people of color, and especially in White-dominant contexts, it causes us tremendous pause as White teachers working toward antiracist goals. If teachers do choose—or are required—to teach this novel, however, we want to offer strategies for helping to ensure that it is taught responsibly and from a critical race perspective. Additionally, we share strategies for discussing the N-word with students in Chapter 6.

image of Whiteness that carries tremendous weight since it is rarely rendered visible through school literary analyses. Making these White literary racial messages evident helps White students understand how Whiteness gets reflected in literature, and how those mirrorings establish and reinforce racial assumptions of superiority in relation to Blackness that work to build and support White privilege and to uphold racism.

Principle 2: Pair White-Authored Views of Racism with Counterstories

As White readers, with school curricula mirroring a sociocultural reality that reinforces a celebratory view of our place in the world, our reading perceptions are very likely skewed if we have not done extensive work examining them critically. We encourage English teachers to foreground the perspectives of people of color as a way to think about how specific canonized stories might look different when told from different racial perspectives. If a class is reading *Huckleberry Finn* or another canonical text by a White author, we suggest the teacher pair that text with a counterstory. As we mentioned in Chapter 1, counterstories are narratives told from the perspective of people of color that call into question problematic racial ideologies, exposing the often invisible or insidious ways that racism works. Counterstories expose Whiteness and disrupt taken-for-granted thinking about race. When the two types of stories are paired together, counterstories can help to make the underlying racial messages of these White-authored, canonical texts more visible.

Principle 3: Ensure Students Understand How a Text *Critiques* Racism

As we argued in Chapter 3 as well, text selection alone will not work to dispel dominant racial ideologies in texts. Such text selections must be accompanied by active efforts to ensure that students understand the racial critiques in those texts—or in the teaching of those texts—lest the literature reinforces existing dominant racial ideologies.

When a text utilizes the satiric mode to deliver its racial critique, this concern is amplified, since irony regularly is missed or misunderstood by many readers. If a reader misses the racial critique of a satiric text, not realizing that it uses irony to criticize its subject(s), the reader leaves the experience either with initial racial assumptions intact or, worse, with additional resources to reinforce problematic racial assumptions. Returning to our treatment of *Huckleberry Finn*, critics have pointed out the way that *scholars* have debated its satiric messages for over a century, making its placement in schools with less savvy readers problematic. For these reasons, teachers need strategies to ensure that students not only tell us they understand how satire works, but show this to us through their writing as well.

Principle 4: Investigate Canonicity with Students

Rather than accepting the canonicity of a text and guiding students to appreciate its *established* merits, teachers can guide students to interrogate the place of a text within the canon. Additionally, when canonical texts—especially those written by White authors—focus on race and racism, teachers can ensure that this investigation of canonicity explores why a particular text might be upheld by White-dominant society as an example of literary greatness. In other words, what might a White-authored canonical text that addresses racism reflect about Whiteness?

Engaging in such tests of canonicity accomplishes multiple goals. First, testing a text's canonicity better aligns literary curriculum with an inquiry focus. As Wiggins and McTighe (2005) argue, curriculum that moves students toward deep, complex "understandings" invites students to grapple with the questions that a discipline considers "essential": without easy answers, debatable, enduring across time, worthy of an adult's knowing. Asking students to investigate the canonicity of any particular text, to unearth political motivations like those shared in this chapter around *Huckleberry Finn*, exposes the constructed and situated nature of any literary canon. Asking students to join teachers in investigating and studying such a process positions students as more active knowledge producers rather than mere passive consumers asked to accept and demonstrate fealty to a literary tradition that may support problematic racial ideologies. To engage students in this work, English teachers might ask:

- How does this book compare with other books from similar eras or on similar themes?
- Looking at the typical canon, whose voices are most often heard? Why might this be?
- How have people responded to the suggestion that this text not be taught? Why might this be?

Exploring canonicity in this way is meant to not only demystify the canon but also explore the relationship between canonization and race.

IN THE CLASSROOM: EXPOSING WHITENESS IN *ADVENTURES OF HUCKLEBERRY FINN*

Exposing Whiteness Through the Whiteness Body Biography

Understanding racism is not only about looking into the lives of people of color; it is also about examining Whiteness in texts, making it visible, discussing it—in all its discomforts to White students. How can we, as English teachers, do this well? In this section, we offer a *Whiteness body biography* as one potential strategy for unearthing messages about Whiteness in relation to our focus text, *Huckleberry Finn*.

Teachers likely recognize the body biography as a strategy for unpacking characterization before asking students to write about character with more nuance (Underwood, 1987). Students start with the outline of a body—possibly one traced from an actual student's body onto butcher paper. Next, students seek character traits and position them strategically on the body outline. For example, students might position feelings in the heart (or the head); actions in the hands or legs; or traits like intelligence in the head. Students are encouraged to be strategic with colors (e.g., red to indicate anger) and symbols (e.g., money symbols to indicate greed) and to seek out nuanced, suggested traits as well as those culled from direct characterization. All traits require textual support.

For the purposes of racial literacy, we recommend utilizing this familiar tool to better understand how a character represents Whiteness. Here are some modifications we recommend in order to focus on racial traits. *Actions* (or *inactions*) tied to race (e.g., helping to hide or disguise Jim) could be identified in the hands or feet. *Thoughts* about characters of color (e.g., about what they do or do not understand) could be placed in the head. When characters *speak up* or *remain silent* around issues of race, such lines could go around the mouth. Students could place *racial feelings* (e.g., of disgust, of superiority or inferiority, of fear, of ambivalence, of empathy) in the heart or the mind. If there is more than one form of Whiteness depicted (e.g., "good White" liberalism, anti-Reconstruction southern Whiteness), students could indicate these differences through different colors.

To frame the exercise, teachers might begin with some pointed inquiry questions. The latter guiding question would be especially effective if teachers included at least two texts focused on racism, with one of those written by and about people of color.

> **Essential question:** What does Whiteness look like?
> **Guiding questions:** Is there only one kind of Whiteness? Does
>   Whiteness look different depending on the author or the author's
>   racial identity?

Since the study of Whiteness might be unfamiliar to some students, we offer additional questions to help students as they think about the text in question.

- What accomplishments do Whites achieve, especially in relation to people of color?

- What expectations do Whites demonstrate, especially in relation to those expectations being available to people of color?
- How do Whites treat people of color?
- How are people of color depicted in relation to Whites (e.g., grateful, resentful)?
- What feelings does the book rally for White characters, especially in relation to people of color?

These questions are meant to help launch this inquiry, rather than be exhaustive. We want to share how such an investigation might look in a study of Huck.

Huck's actions in relation to Jim (hands, feet)

- Huck places a snake in Jim's blanket that bites Jim and sickens him horribly. *Whites as heartless or insensitive to what could happen to Blacks physically.*
- Huck plans myriad ploys for discovering information to help him accompany and then free Jim (e.g., dresses up as a girl to listen for information on his alleged death at Pap's hands). *Blacks need Whites, are dependent on Whites, to succeed, to achieve freedom.*
- Huck participates in Tom's plans to extend Jim's capture through all the invented struggles Jim would need to perform as a captive. *Whites go along with other Whites' plans to complicate—or worsen—Black lives, even when those plans are inhumane.*

Huck's thoughts about Jim (head)

- Huck sees Jim as foolishly superstitious in his stories about his beliefs in witches, or misunderstanding of the story of King Solomon. *Whites as more intelligent than Blacks.*
- Huck tricks Jim into thinking he got lost during the fog. *Whites believe we are cleverer than Blacks, who can be duped easily.*
- Huck believes that Jim does not see through the Duke and King's frauds. *Whites as more discerning than Blacks, who do not recognize fraud as easily.*

Huck's words (mouth)

- When Aunt Sally asked Huck if anyone was injured in the steamboat explosion, he replied, "No'm. Killed a nigger," to which Aunt Sally replied, "Well, it's lucky because sometimes people do get hurt." *Whites do not see Blacks as human.*

Huck's racial feelings (heart)

- Huck empathizes with Jim's regrets about hitting his daughter before realizing she was deaf. *Whites as capable of seeing Black humanity.*
- Huck commits to helping Jim flee slavery even if it means going to hell. *Whites will put ourselves in (spiritual) jeopardy to assist Black freedom.*

Some of these traits of Whiteness are contradictory. For example, Huck's racial portrait in relation to Jim shows him to love and care for Jim and to think of him as human, *and* to see him as less intelligent as a Black man—even less intelligent than a White *boy*. Inviting students to note such complexity will help build analysis skills that are more attuned to contradictions in character in general. And again, we want to point to a range of interpretations of such scenes, some which differ greatly from those we offer here (see Chadwick-Joshua, 1998).

After some initial investigations of White traits in texts, teachers might help students begin to synthesize how Whiteness is portrayed overall, using the details added to the body biography to assist. Teachers could turn to the essential and guiding questions above for this synthesis work. But if that process feels difficult, we offer some sentence starters to further guide students.

- To help students identify facets of Whiteness: When (character name) __(verb)_____, we see Whiteness as (a trait) _____.
- To help students name a facet of Whiteness: Whiteness (verb) _____.

If using the term *Whiteness* proves too abstract, turn back to the term *Whites* to explore how Whiteness is portrayed in the text, as we did above in the list of possible details to consider for making Whiteness visible in the text.

A culminating activity for bringing this exercise together is to help students compile the portrait of Whiteness presented in the book overall. Teachers could bring students back to the suggested essential question: What does Whiteness look like? To respond, students might point to many of the claims that our research exposed. Whites see themselves as helpful to Black people, to the point of self-sacrifice, in noble terms. Whites are wily, intelligent, and resourceful, in the interests of helping Black people. Whites come to important realizations about social issues like slavery through their humanity, their ability to empathize with Black people. Also important to point out is how Blackness, and Black people, are portrayed *in order for* this portrait of Whiteness to become visible. Blacks are less intelligent and discerning of others' culpability, especially, but also about cultural stories (e.g., of King Solomon), thereby needing the help of Whites to change their life circumstances. To be clear, when we propose a focus on unearthing Whiteness in this text, it is *not* to re-center Whiteness within an already White-centered curriculum. Rather, we aim to help White teachers see how the texts we choose *toward antiracist goals* make us look, as White people, racially, in ways that work against such intentions.

Comparing *Huckleberry Finn* with a Counterstory

Extending the example of *Huckleberry Finn*, teachers might consider pairing the novel with Chestnutt's "The Passing of Grandison" (1898/2001). Chestnutt, a Black author and contemporary of Twain who also published in journals like *The Atlantic Monthly*, took the topic of slavery and the desire to escape its bonds and rendered a story that reads very differently from Twain's. We offer a summary, with spoilers of the story, to set up a possible exercise for teachers, but highly recommend that teachers read the story themselves first.

In "Grandison," Dick Owens, a White son of a wealthy slave owner, wants to win the hand of his love, Charity Lomax. But she wants him to do something important first, agreeing with assessments of him as lazy and "good for nothing." Somewhat inspired by the recent arrest and imprisonment of a local White man who helped to free the slave of a vicious slaveholder, Dick suggests to Charity that he could do the same with a slave of his father's. Although she doubts the likelihood of Dick doing anything at all, she agrees to hear him out after he tries the plan. Dick presents his father with the idea of taking a trip up North with one of the slaves as a manservant, suggesting a slave he thought would likely flee with the opportunity. Instead, Colonel Owens recommends he take Grandison, an obsequious slave who says he'd be worried about abolitionists' efforts to take him from his happy place on the Owens estate. This statement seals the deal for the Colonel: "'I allow he's abolitionist proof.'" Once in the North, Dick cannot shake Grandison, who remains at his side despite increasingly direct suggestions about the opportunity to flee, until they get to Canada and Grandison disappears. Dick returns to Kentucky to tell his father—and Charity, who agrees to marry him—only to have Grandison return after three weeks with grand tales of being kidnapped by abolitionists. Although Dick suggests to the Colonel that Grandison's story might be far-fetched, the Colonel hears exactly the kind of devotion and support for slavery on the part of Blacks that he wants to hear. And then, soon thereafter, Grandison, together with his entire family and wife, escapes to Canada: "And strangely enough, the underground railroad seemed to have had its tracks cleared and signals set for this particular train" (p. 281).

In "Grandison," Chestnutt honors the roles of Blacks in effecting their own freedom by performing a false and strategic servitude and devotion to

Whites, and exposes White ambivalence to Blackness, and White inanity and cruelty through slavery. Chestnutt's story also utilizes irony, making it a fruitful text to use in relation to Twain's. Additionally, the Common Core State Standards for 11–12th grades include a reading literature standard that would nicely wed these two texts: "Demonstrate knowledge of 18th, 19th, and early-20th-century foundational works of American literature, including how two or more texts from the same period treat similar themes or topics." Teachers easily could use this pairing to explore how Twain and Chestnutt treat Blacks' roles in escaping slavery and the portrayal of White slaveholders. But we also could imagine even more nuanced comparisons, as you will see from the starter quotations and comparisons in Table 4.1.

Students could begin this analysis by identifying a central textual detail through a quotation that allows them to draw comparisons between characters from each text. Table 4.1 aims to show a range of possible comparisons between the texts as starting points, with the idea that students be asked to pursue the comparison of two characters or groups of characters more fully across the texts. To show how this process might look, we begin with examining how Twain and Chestnutt render Black male slaves. In the quotation from Chestnutt listed in the table, we hear Grandison's response to being invited to accompany Dick to the North. "'Dey won't try ter steal me, will dey, marster?' asked the negro, with sudden alarm." To the left of the quote, students could consider how Jim's characterization looks in relation to this quotation. Like Grandison in this quotation, Jim appears trusting of Whites like Huck, earnestly so, succumbing to their judgments. For Grandison, this comment to Colonel Owens shows how capably Grandison can perform the kind of fealty his master expects of servants, but one that he utters strategically to build his master's trust in him in order to effect the eventual escape not only of himself but his entire family. (Note that Chadwick-Joshua's [1998] reading of *Huckleberry Finn* matches portrayals of Black and White characters in Chestnutt's story.)

There is so much more to compare in these two texts. After a thorough comparison of characters, teachers could ask how different texts tell different stories of our nation. Students might consider how American literature portrays Black slaves differently, with some Black authors exposing assumed fealty as strategic subterfuge. Students also might notice how the two authors both use satire to critique southern slaveholders and their gentility, with subtle differences. Such realizations would go far to engage students in thinking through literature toward antiracist goals.

Teachers motivated to complicate canonical portraits of racism with texts by and about people of color might extend their searches past literature to visual art and other media. We include just a few possibilities here to get the process started.

Table 4.1. Comparing Huck Finn and Grandison

Twain's *Huckleberry Finn*		Chestnutt's "Grandison"
How does "Grandison" connect to *Huckleberry Finn*?	What story does the counterstory tell? Which key scenes help us to see the significance of these differences?	How does *Huckleberry Finn* connect to "Grandison"?
Characterization of Jim	"'Dey won't try ter steal me, will dey, marster?' asked the negro, with sudden alarm" (p. 273).	Characterization of Grandison
Characterization of southern gentry/ plantation owners	"The colonel was beaming. This [Grandison's demonstration of fealty to his master before the trip North] was true gratitude, and his feudal heart thrilled at such appreciative homage. What cold-blooded, heartless monsters they were who would break up this blissful relationship of kindly protection on the one hand, of wise subordination and loyal dependence on the other! The colonel always became indignant at the mere thought of such wickedness" (p. 272).	Characterization of the colonel
Characterization of Huck	"'I confess,' he [Dick Owens] admitted, 'that while my principles were against the prisoner [the white man accused and convicted of aiding a slave escape his master], my sympathies were on his side'" (p. 269).	Characterization of Dick Owens
Characterization of Pap	"'Except that I do hate,' she [Charity] added, relenting slightly, 'to see a really clever man so utterly lazy and good for nothing'" (p. 270).	Characterization of Dick Owens

Portraits by Kehinde Wiley. Following President Obama's selection of Wiley as the artist to render his presidential portrait for posterity, teachers may recognize his name and visual style. A Black artist who grew up in Los Angeles and studied at Yale, Wiley creates paintings in the style of Old Master portraits of famous, powerful, White leaders, disrupting them through the centering of Black bodies in hip-hop attire in these visually potent stances. A rich comparative exercise to mirror the literary comparisons suggested above might juxtapose Wiley's "Napoleon Leading the Army over the Alps" (2005) with the original he revises, Jacques-Louis David's "Napoleon Crossing the Alps" (1801). We could even see using the format in Table 4.1 in comparable ways, citing visual details in the center and asking students to analyze how they compare across the works. Some questions to follow might include: How are the stances of the two subjects similar? What messages do these stances convey about the subject? How do the clothing choices for each artist contribute to the message? What about the use of the horse, especially an 1801 use versus one in 2005? Overall, what does it mean to center a Black man on a horse dressed in a popular brand of construction boots, long athletic shorts, and a bandana on his head in this well-known image from a "master"? Again, we would ask students to consider how racial identity affects the stories told about power, nobility or glory, and being American. We can see such an examination bolstering the work of a *Huckleberry Finn* unit in complex, sophisticated ways.

Sketches on Saturday Night Live. *Saturday Night Live* (SNL) created a race-based version of its successful Jeopardy! skit with Black Jeopardy! The premise of this newer skit, which began in 2014, is that the host plus two of the three contestants share a common, lower-middle-class, American Black experience through which the contestants successfully respond to the host's questions. The third, rotating contestant is typically a White person who thinks he or she understands American Blackness but does not. In a post–*Black Panther* episode, the show positioned Chadwick Boseman as his character T'Challa, responding with Wakanda optimism to the questions offered by host Kenan Thompson. Although an SNL sketch may seem a strange suggestion for a unit on Twain, we could imagine students extending their consideration of how Black artists utilize satire to expose racism. In a typical SNL Black Jeopardy! skit, questions and answers follow a Black gaze or perspective, rendering Whites or non-American Blacks outsiders. How does the skit expose Whiteness? How does it situate a particular kind of Blackness that is typically not the focus of a show like Jeopardy!, which presumes to focus on "common" knowledge worthy of an astute American's ken?

The American literary curriculum has proven remarkably resistant to significant changes in text selection for over a century. Building a curriculum that features counterstories *in relation* to canonical, White-authored texts offers teachers one way to begin to break down this White textual monopoly as a means of offering students a robust, antiracist curriculum worthy of careful study.

Solidifying Satire's Aims for Readers

Given satire's purpose to expose social ills, teachers must ensure that students understand these aims well. When the satiric text chosen aims at exposing racism, it is crucial to reinforce interpretive practices that bring attention to the ways satire works, as well as to the potential misreadings it could trigger. We recommend a few key steps for doing this work.

First, we recommend clear, direct instruction about what satire is and why an author utilizes satire as the mode of narrative delivery. To bolster our own understandings, we turned to Sharon Hamilton's *Essential Literary Terms* (2016). Satire delivers social critique via humor that is sometimes light and sometimes far more scathing. Of course, there are different types of satire, including direct (addressing its audience as a sympathetic listener) and indirect (the more typical, implied audience), as well as Horatian (light mockery) versus Juvenalian (scathing) and others. Satirists utilize verbal irony, which is more closely related to the language used, as well as structural irony, which pervades the work, often through a naive narrator who misunderstands some or much of what is being narrated. Sharing some of these details, with examples, so students can deepen their understandings is an important beginning. It can be done by asking students to identify which approaches Twain and others use, as well as to consider why those authors might use those and with what effects.

It is also important for students to understand the pleasures and the risks of employing satire. For discerning readers, the pleasures of engaging with satire abound since recognizing what an author is *really* doing in making ironic statements can be enjoyed as a reward for a reader's careful attention and knowledge. Such understandings are meant as flattery between a knowing writer and his or her expected reader. Hamilton also attends to the possible shock of a naive reader who misses the message. What happens when a reader—a student in our classes—mistakes a racial critique for direct racism in the text?

Wiggins and McTighe (2005) explain that new, complex knowledge often gets misunderstood by students just beginning to build their understandings of a topic. For teachers who understand this part of the learning process, looking out for such misunderstandings affords a keen opportunity to show students that they are on the right track, but have not quite achieved full, adroit understanding. We recommend attending to such potential misunderstandings involving satire by explicitly evaluating the site of critique. Teachers might ask students to do this analysis in two steps. First, the teacher asks students, What's so funny? Who and/or what is being targeted? What, if anything, is the author trying to correct? How?

For example, early in *Huckleberry Finn*, in a key scene in Chapter 6, Pap is drunk and telling Huck about the problems of an American government that permits a Black man to live a better life than he lives himself. The entire two long paragraphs beginning with "Call this a govment!" work for this exercise, but for brevity's sake, we focus on analyzing only the second paragraph, cited in full here.

Oh, yes, this is a wonderful govment, wonderful. Why, looky here. There was a free nigger there, from Ohio, a mulatter, most as white as a white man. He had the whitest shirt on you ever see, too, and the shiniest hat; and there ain't a man in that town that's got as fine clothes as what he had; and he had a gold watch and chain, and a silver-headed cane—the awfulest old gray-headed nabob in the State. And what do you think? They said he was a p'fessor in a college, and could talk all kinds of languages, and knowed everything. And that ain't the wust. They said he could *vote*, when he was at home. Well, that let me out. Thinks I, what is the country a-coming to? It was 'lection day, and I was just about to go and vote, myself, if I warn't too drunk to get there; but when they told me there was a State in this country where they'd let that nigger vote, I drawed out. I says I'll never vote agin. Them's the very words I said; they all heard me; and the country may rot for all me—I'll never vote agin as long as I live. And to see the cool way of that nigger—why, he wouldn't a give me the road if I hadn't shoved him out o' the way. I says to the people, why ain't this nigger put up at auction and sold?—that's what I want to know. And what do you reckon they said? Why, they said he couldn't be sold till he'd been in the State six months, and he hadn't been there that long yet. There, now—that's a specimen. They call that a govment that can't sell a free nigger till he's been in the State six months. Here's a govment that calls itself a govment, and lets on to be a govment, and thinks it is a govment, and yet's got to set stock-still for six whole months before it can take ahold of a prowling, thieving, infernal, white-shirted free nigger, and—.

Pap doesn't finish his speech because he falls into a tub of salt pork, extending the scene's humor.

Teachers could guide students to see how Twain uses indirect, Horatian satire to expose the inanity of Pap's fury over the Black man's clean clothing, opulent accessories, literacy, knowledge of multiple languages, voting rights, and right to remain free (for 6 months) even while in a slave state. Students could be helped to note how Twain's satiric humor mocks Pap for several reasons. First, Pap calls this upright citizen a "prowling, thieving, infernal" person, when those labels more accurately describe Pap, thieving from his own son. Second, Pap thinks it terrible that the man is so knowledgeable, with extensive formal education, reminding us that he found Huck to be too uppity as a result of his schooling as well. Third, Pap balks at the fact that the Black man has the power to vote, leading Pap to affirm his commitment never to vote again, something he did not do this day because he was too drunk anyway. Additionally, Pap suggests that the Black man was impolite not to move out of Pap's way, *requiring* Pap to push him out of the way, showing the reverse: that Pap, and not the Black man, is horribly uncouth. Finally, when Pap complains that the U.S. government fails when it makes it impossible to *sell* a *free* Black man, Pap exposes how little he understands the law. Through this passage, Twain's ironic humor targets ignorant, racist, poor White Americans furious over the successes of Black people flourishing under greater racial equality—Whites who attempt to affirm their racial superiority to Blacks. Twain does this while exposing the groundless, laughable nature of such perspectives.

In addition to this first layer of literary analysis, we recommend a second to better ensure that students understand the satire. After naming the target of satire through reference to textual details, students must explicitly identify what *some* readers might *misunderstand* if they did not realize what the author was doing. It is also important for students to explicitly name what would be at stake in such misunderstandings. Finally, students could explain how they knew their satiric reading was correct.

So, in the Twain passage above, readers who do not register the satiric critique, might be *following* Pap's complaints about the Black man and the U.S. government rather than *laughing* at them. As savvy readers, we know that Twain is making fun of Pap, and not critiquing the Black man that Pap is talking about in his rant, nor is Twain critiquing the U.S. government. A naive reader may miss the fact that Twain does not intend to *critique* the U.S. government for offering freedom and voting rights to Blacks in some states, but rather to critique those states that do *not* offer these rights and privileges to Black people. As outrageous as such misreadings might sound to astute readers, teachers might recall how Arac (1997/2004) reminded us of the ways that the satiric 1970s show "All in the Family" was enjoyed by *opposing* sides of racial and gender debates.

At stake in such a misreading would be a deepening of racist thinking in the reader rather than the racial critique Twain intended. A less sophisticated reader might miss the political critique aimed at states still holding to racist practices via slavery. As savvy readers, we know that Twain is making fun of Pap, and not critiquing the Black man or the U.S. government, because Pap's behavior throughout the novel has been reprehensible: physically abusing Huck, taking Huck's money, taking Huck away from a loving family in order to make Pap's own life easier (and more inebriated). Twain would not want a reader to trust such a character.

When we have previewed these teaching strategies for satire and for *Huckleberry Finn* in particular, teachers have appreciated the very "literary" focus of the unit. What we make sure to point out to teachers, though, is that if they focus *only* on satire, students will miss a key form of critique or race-based analysis that we have argued for throughout this chapter: an examination of how the novel relies on existing, circulating representations of Whites as racially heroic, superior to the Blacks we honorably want to help. We hope that the vantage points offered in this chapter offer teachers the resources and resolve to take this extra analytic step with texts like Twain's to move us all closer to antiracist teaching goals.

Considering *Huckleberry Finn's* Place in the Canon
from a Critical Race Perspective

We have seen essential questions for *Huckleberry Finn* such as, Should this novel be taught in schools? While this phrasing of the question aims to investigate canonicity, it also does so in a somewhat disingenuous manner. The book *is* being taught in schools, so the curriculum is offering an implicit response to the question rather clearly. Rather than posit something of a false or counterfeit question, we recommend inflecting such a question of canonicity with a racial twist. What if a unit asked students to consider, *What racial feelings does this text uphold? Why might* this *be the book that American schools choose, especially as a text that represents race and racism?*

Of course, as many readers and critics affirm, the canonicity of *Huckleberry Finn* is based on literary merit. Eliot described it as a "masterpiece." Hemingway proclaimed that all American literature grows out of this novel (as long as you ignore the ending). What we did not realize when setting out to investigate the teaching of this novel is that its positioning as a literary masterpiece was politically motivated.

Literary scholars trace the American canonicity of *Huckleberry Finn* to the post–World War II 1950s. According to Arac (1997/2004), it was Lionel Trilling, who would become one of the most notable cultural and literary critics of his time, who in 1948 wrote an essay about the importance of American literature in the first edition of *Literary History of the United States*. Part of Trilling's efforts to define the American literary and cultural moment included positioning *Huckleberry Finn* on the shelf alongside other texts in the Great Books tradition:

> *Huckleberry Finn* served a national and global political function as an icon of integration, and the importance of this cultural work overrode the offense the book generated among many of its newly authorized, but also newly obligated, African American readers. (Arac, 1997/2004, p. 440)

In short, this novel's stature in the literary world was born in the mix of a postwar nationalism. The United States was seeking to imagine itself as far more egalitarian—especially around racial equity—than reality sustains. Additionally, because this book is claimed to be unequivocally "American," any questions about its merits unsettle a questioner's "Americanness." So, as much as its literary merit, *Huckleberry Finn's* fantasy story of loving support between White and Black Americans is part of what propelled this text into the canonical mainstream.

Arac (1997/2004) discusses the structure of feelings generated for White readers by *Huckleberry Finn* through Longinus's notion of the sublime. According to Longinus:

The sublime produces, and depends on, a series of identifications, so that the words of a character, at a sublime moment, seem "the echo of a great soul" that is the author's, and in reading the sublime we are "uplifted . . . as if we had ourselves produced" what we hear or read. . . . The key Greek term here is *ekstasis*, a getting out of one's place, a "transport" into a new state or position. (p. 454)

Arac argues that, in moments like the scene where Huck decides to go to hell, White readers, especially, feel the sublime, joining themselves as readers with Huck and Twain in this imagined unification. Arac explains the effects of experiencing such sublime moments:

Readers may then tend to be highly protective of the characters and authors in which they are invested, and at the same time will feel themselves intimately threatened by anything that seems to criticize or diminish either Huck or Twain. (p. 454)

This type of analysis can help students begin to understand a relationship between this novel, the literary canon, and Whiteness.

CONCLUSION

This book as a whole, and this chapter in particular, encourages teachers to be racially literate enough to see when our proclivities as White readers "unintentionally" perpetuate racism as we strive to teach our students to love literature. The emphasis on "good Whites" here points to the problematic ways that White people *want* to be seen in racial contexts like the one portrayed in Twain's text. What we hope becomes evident in this chapter and throughout the book is that, without substantive changes in the ways we teach the texts we choose or are required to teach, such racial desires will be insufficient without the necessary work of also understanding how to strategically *read* such texts *differently*.

CHAPTER 5

Applying a Critical Race Theory Lens to Literary Analysis

In the previous two chapters, we argued that both *different reading* and *reading differently* (Morrell, 2018) are important for building racial literacy. We have been slowly laying out, across our chapters, a range of entry points for antiracist literature instruction. In this chapter, we offer another "way in" by articulating a critical race theory (CRT) lens that English teachers can use to lead their students in a critical race analysis of any text.

COMMON CHALLENGE:
REINFORCING RACISM VIA TRADITIONAL LITERARY ANALYSIS

Ms. Allen taught 9th-grade English in a predominantly White and affluent community in rural Michigan. Midway through the year, she was required to teach a unit on *To Kill a Mockingbird* using a New Critical approach for literary analysis. New Criticism, a formalist approach that views the text as an object separate from context, is easily recognizable as the most common method of literary analysis in U.S. schools (Applebee, 1993). It focuses on close reading and examination of literary elements, such as theme, plot, character, and symbol. As is often the case in a New Critical analysis of *To Kill a Mockingbird*, Ms. Allen and her students discussed the main symbol of the book, the mockingbird:

> *Sam:* It's a sin to kill a mockingbird.
> *Ms. Allen:* Why?
> *Sam:* They don't do anything bad.
> *Ms. Allen:* And if you're killing a mockingbird, something that hasn't done anything wrong, that can't defend itself, it's worse than killing something that has its own defense. How does this add to Atticus's moral character?
> *Student:* (Inaudible)
> *Ms. Allen:* Yes, he's an advocate for those . . . and who is he in this case being an advocate for?

Students: Tom Robinson.

Ms. Allen: Tom Robinson could be a mockingbird, but what is it a *symbol* for?

Rachel: The Black race.

Ms. Allen: So our mockingbird is someone who can't defend himself, who is innocent. At this point we don't know if Tom Robinson is a mockingbird or not, but we know that Atticus is an advocate because [Tom] can't defend himself.

This is, in many ways, a pretty typical New Critical analysis of the symbol of the mockingbird. But even before beginning this unit, Ms. Allen expressed concern that this traditional analysis characterized Tom Robinson, a symbol of the "Black race," as a defenseless victim, thereby reinforcing stereotypes about White heroes and Black victims. Ultimately, Ms. Allen revised her approach to read against the novel in ways that have taught both authors of this book a lot about antiracist literature study (e.g., Borsheim-Black, 2015). In the next sections, we unpack this teaching scenario in more depth and propose a CRT lens as a tool for deepening literary analysis around the issues of race and racism.

WHY THIS MATTERS FROM AN ANTIRACIST PERSPECTIVE

In previous chapters, we have explored the racism inherent in literature curriculum that prioritizes White-authored texts generally and White-authored texts on the topic of racism specifically. We have argued that it is a system of forces, not simply individual teachers' selections, that cement a White-dominated literature curriculum in place for decades. Here, we look at the other side of the coin—at the ways we *analyze* those texts—to examine ways that typical literary analysis can reinforce racism as well, despite English teachers' desire to do the opposite. The opening scenario, Ms. Allen's concerns, and ample research all suggest that New Critical readings of *To Kill a Mockingbird* and other canonical White-authored texts about racism actually can reinforce rather than interrupt racism (e.g., Boyd, 2002; Dressel, 2005; Thein, 2011).

In response, English educators have called for critical approaches to literary analysis that help students engage more directly with power, privilege, and oppression (e.g., Anagnostopoulos, 2010; Beach et al., 2008; Dyches, 2018). If English teachers take a critical approach to "reading against" texts, even canonical novels can provide rich ground for teaching students about power and oppression (Macaluso & Macaluso, 2018). Ms. Allen was familiar with and interested in taking a more critical approach, but the decision was not entirely her own. As a new member of the department, she felt pressure to conform to the department's expectations for traditional literary analysis. Specifically, the common assessment for the unit asked students to write a character analysis, which necessitated a New Critical approach. Departmental expectations to teach from a New Critical perspective constitute what Berchini (2016) calls "structuring contexts" that limit the extent to which a teacher's antiracist efforts can be effected. These structuring contexts made implementing a critical race analysis challenging for Ms. Allen, especially as a new teacher at the school.

Acknowledging both the systems in place that make change difficult for English teachers and the limitations of a New Critical approach for antiracist literature instruction, we offer the CRT lens. It is a tool English teachers can use—even with texts they are already teaching—to support students in reading these texts differently, with the ultimate goal of developing both literary analysis skills and racial literacy.

WHAT YOU CAN DO: APPLY A CRT LENS TO LITERARY ANALYSIS

Just as a feminist lens directs focus on representations of gender in literature, a CRT lens directs focus on representations of race in literature. If feminism asks the overarching question, How does this text represent gender? a CRT lens asks, How does this text represent race? With this question central to literary interpretation, seeing, naming, and analyzing the role of race in literature become unavoidable.

In general terms, the CRT lens offers a set of questions that we have organized around literary elements. Table 5.1 presents questions, divided into three levels, each of which is designed to take students deeper into a critical race analysis of the text. We explain each of the levels in more detail in discussing the principles below.

We envision the CRT lens as complementary to other approaches to literary analysis, including New Criticism. In other words, we would not suggest the CRT lens as a substitution for New Critical analysis or even as the *only* tool for literary analysis. We see it as one tool English teachers might use in their efforts to carry out antiracist literature instruction.

And, to be clear, taking up tenets of CRT to analyze literature is not new; college-level scholarship has engaged in such literary interpretation for decades. But this approach has yet to reach the teaching of literature at the secondary level in ways that would bolster our field's efforts to address racism *before* students get to college. Additionally, although we offer one way to consolidate CRT tenets to take up such a critical position, this is not the only way. For teachers who have wanted to engage deeply with literature around race representations but were not sure where to begin, this chapter carefully presents a way to do so.

Table 5.1. CRT Lens

Literary Elements	Questions for Racializing Literary Elements
Characterization	Who are the central and secondary characters of the text?
	How are characters of color portrayed? Are they central or minor characters? Round or flat? Static or dynamic? Is their racial identity named or left assumed? How are White characters portrayed, especially in relation to characters of color? Are they central or minor characters? Round, flat, static, or dynamic? Is their racial identity named or left assumed? How does race intersect with other categories of difference? When race is considered in relation to other categories of difference (e.g., gender, sexuality, age, ability), how is race affected?
	How does characterization reflect racial ideology? Does the story rely on White savior characters? To what extent does the text reflect or challenge racial stereotypes of Whiteness or Blackness?
Setting	What are the settings (e.g., social, historical, legal) of the text?
	What are the racial dynamics of this setting? How does the text represent racial dynamics of the setting?
	What does the setting reveal about the racial ideologies of the text?
Plot	What are central conflicts in the text?
	To what extent is race a factor in those conflicts?
	How do complex understandings of racism explain the trajectory of the plot and its central conflicts?
Theme	What are central themes of the text?
	What messages about race and racism are conveyed through these themes?
	To what extent does the text represent these themes in complex or stereotypical racial terms? What do the themes reveal about the racial ideology of the text?
Point of View	From what perspective is the story written or told?
	How does the racial perspective through which the story is told affect the story? If it's a story told from the perspective of a person of color, what details of a racialized experience does it highlight? If it's a story told from a White perspective, what details of a racialized experience (of Whiteness) does it highlight?
	If it is a story told from the perspective of a person of color, to what extent does this story function as a counterstory to interrupt dominant ways of thinking about race/ism? If it is a White-authored text, to what extent does it reflect dominant racial ideology?

Principle 1: Begin with Familiar Literary Elements

Throughout the book, we have relied on familiar pedagogical principles and practices to merge antiracist goals with literature curriculum and instruction (e.g., backward design and the use of assessments to anchor critical learning in a unit toward racial literacy objectives). Once again, we return to the familiar—analysis of literary elements—to tie teaching about race and racism to the ways literature instruction is often done English classrooms. The first level of questions simply asks students to begin by identifying central characters, conflicts, setting, and point of view in the novel.

Principle 2: Racialize Literary Elements

The second level of questions asks students to racialize those literary elements. For each literary element (e.g., characterization, setting, etc.) we inflect typical, New Critical interpretive questions with race to help students consider literary elements in racialized terms. The goal at this level is to identify racial aspects of the text—whether they are represented explicitly or implicitly.

Principle 3: Consider Racial Implications of Literary Analysis

As a means of synthesizing complex literary analysis, English teachers regularly ask students to consider, So what? Why does this matter? Questions in the third level of Table 5.1 help students answer questions of significance by guiding them toward the racial implications of their analysis of literary elements: What is the racial ideology of the text?

Principle 4: Leverage Complex Race Concepts to Deepen Literary Interpretation

Critical race analysis requires students to draw on complex understandings of how racism works using key race concepts that explain its functioning. What teachers and students need in order to respond to these questions is a bedrock of racial literacy from which to draw, to help identify a range of patterns in a text's depiction of race and racism. Just as analysis through a feminist lens requires an understanding of key concepts, like patriarchy or gender discrimination or objectification, for example, analysis through a CRT lens requires understanding of some key concepts as well. We have listed and defined some of important ones here.

Terms for Identifying Levels of Racism. Most people can easily identify overt examples of individual/interpersonal racism. But, of course, racism is not always overt or obvious. To support students in developing a more complex understanding of racism, it can be helpful to equip them with language for identifying racism at different levels.

- **Individual/interpersonal racism.** This term refers to the attitudes and behaviors of individual people, including prejudice (racist attitudes), discrimination (behaving in ways that disadvantage people), or even implicit bias (racist attitudes that are unknown even to the individual holding them). It can be overt or covert.
- **Systemic racism.** Systemic racism is reflected in the inequity of systems or institutions that shape daily life, like the legal system, the educational system, housing, employment, health care, politics, or wealth.
- **Ideological racism.** Ideology refers to the ideas or ideals on which people base their view of the world. Ideological racism refers to the structuring of people's thinking based on White supremacy.

Terms for Understanding Colorblindness. Thinking about racism on an ideological level is quite complex for many students. What does that mean? What does that look like? Bonilla-Silva (2013) argues that colorblindness is the dominant racial ideology in the United States. As we explained in Chapter 1, colorblindness describes the various rationales White people use to distance themselves from being perceived as racist while still upholding racist beliefs, behaviors, institutions, and systems. In his work, Bonilla-Silva (2013) breaks colorblindness down into four different types. These terms can be useful for thinking about how racism works in more covert ways.

- **Naturalization.** Naturalization, just like it sounds, suggests that racism is a natural occurrence. For example, if White people claim that neighborhoods are segregated because White people just prefer to be with people who feel familiar to them, or that people segregate themselves by race because that is "just the way things are," they are drawing on naturalization. These ideas suggest biological bases, not racism, as an explanation for segregation.
- **Abstract liberalism.** As we explained in Chapter 1, this type of colorblindness has to do with using values of liberalism, like equal opportunity, meritocracy, individualism, or free choice, and turning them around to explain race-related issues in ways that deny realities of systemic racism. This type of colorblindness suggests that if inequality exists, it is a result of the individual choices people make in their lives. It ignores the role of systemic racism in the lives of people of color.
- **Minimization.** This type of colorblindness suggests that racism is not as bad as it once was, that it is no longer a significant factor in the lives of people of color. It is recognizable when White people

claim people of color are "just too sensitive," should "just get over it," or are "playing the race card."

- **Cultural racism.** This type of colorblindness references or blames characteristics of a racial group as explanations for inequality; for example, saying that Black parents are not as involved as White parents in their children's education.

Terms for Understanding Racial Perspective. In literature, the racial perspective from which a story is told is important. In order to fully appreciate the importance of perspective, it is helpful to be familiar with a few key concepts.

- **Stock stories.** CRT scholars explain that people of the dominant racial group, White people, tell and retell "stock stories" in an effort to impose a view of the world based on our own racial perspective. In White people's version of the story, Delgado (1989) explains, we attempt to avoid blame or responsibility for our role in social inequality. We repeat these stock stories again and again until they become canonized, until they are taken for granted as reality or as *the* story.
- **White savior narratives.** White savior narratives are kinds of stock stories. The term *White savior narrative* is used to describe stories that feature good White people "saving the day" for people of color. They are problematic to the extent that they override the role people of color have played and continue to play in their own active resistance against racism. White savior narratives are common; students might recognize other examples from popular media, like *The Green Book, Dangerous Minds, Freedom Writers, The Blind Side,* or *The Help.* They are also persuasive—because they often reflect White people's desires to be perceived as "good White people." These stories have more to do with establishing the morality of White characters than with the lives and experiences of characters of color (e.g., Morrison, 1992).
- **Counterstories.** As we explained in Chapter 4, counterstories challenge stock stories as acts of resistance. Counterstories are stories and versions of stories that are not often told; they feature perspectives of people whose voices historically have been marginalized or silenced. They call into question problematic racial ideologies, exposing the often invisible or insidious ways that racism works. While stock stories contribute to the notion that the dominance of Whiteness is normal and natural, counterstories expose Whiteness in a way that makes it more visible.

IN THE CLASSROOM: APPLYING A CRT LENS TO
TO KILL A MOCKINGBIRD

In this section, we apply the CRT lens to an analysis of *To Kill a Mockingbird*. We chose *To Kill a Mockingbird* as the focus of this chapter and for the demonstration of this lens for a couple of reasons. First, it is one of the most commonly taught texts in U.S. schools (Applebee, 1993), which means that many, many English teachers ask us about tackling themes of racism in this novel. Second, we chose it because we find the racial messages of this text to be complex and, at times, contradictory, making it a very difficult novel to teach from a critical race perspective. The CRT lens helps to name those contradictions.

Character

Main characters, of course, include Atticus, Scout, Jem, Calpurnia, Aunt Alexandra, Dill, Boo Radley, Tom Robinson, and a whole host of other secondary characters too numerous to mention, most of whom are White.

How are characters of color portrayed? The two main characters of color, Tom Robinson and Calpurnia, are much less developed than White characters in the novel. Although one of the main themes revolves around racism and although the main conflict hinges on Tom's character, Tom himself remains, in many ways, a secondary character—secondary to Atticus and the Finch children. In fact, readers see or hear very little from Tom. He has little agency to act on his own behalf in the course of his trial. Rather, it is Atticus Finch, a White attorney, who is the main character, the hero, and ultimately a cultural icon. Atticus is celebrated for taking on Tom's case even though they all know a fair trial is impossible.

What does this analysis reveal to readers about the underlying racial ideology of the text? Given both the marginalization of characters of color and the celebration of Atticus Finch's role as the White hero, many readers consider *To Kill a Mockingbird* to be an example of a White savior narrative. This analysis is significant, because it emphasizes that this story has more to do with White characters' experiences with and responses to racism than it does with the characters of color. It signals to readers that the story reflects White perspectives and therefore likely dominant White racial ideology.

The lens also asks students to consider the characterization of White characters, especially in relation to characters of color. This analysis could focus on one of any number of White characters in this novel. Rather than focus our analysis on one White character, however, we have decided to think about how White characters are represented generally. To do so, we turn our attention here to a scene that is central to the development of White characters in the novel: the scene where Scout accidentally persuades the angry lynch mob to disperse from outside Tom's jail cell. Once again, this scene focuses not on Tom's experience inside the jail but on White characters' responses to overt racism outside. Scout disrupts the lynching with innocent humor; Atticus puts himself in harm's way to defend Tom; and Mr. Cunningham has a change of heart and encourages the other men to go home. While Mr. Cunningham showed up prepared to murder Tom, he left the scene with his humanity intact, still a good person.

How does this characterization reflect racial ideology? We argue that this scene excuses individuals' overt racism in ways that preserve the possibility that these are still good White people *regardless* of their actions. Given this satisfying ending for White characters—an ending that differs from many, many historical examples of lynchings—the novel may allow White readers to distance themselves from racism, to celebrate themselves as good White people believing that they, like Atticus, also would do the right thing in those circumstances (e.g., Macaluso, 2017).

This analysis of White characters makes visible the fact that White authors often perpetuate dominant White racial ideologies, especially in accounts of racism.

Setting

To Kill a Mockingbird is set in the fictional town of Maycomb, Alabama, during Jim Crow. Many people have suggested that events in *To Kill a Mockingbird* were inspired by the Scottsboro Affair (e.g., Sigward, 2014), referring to the story of nine Black teenage boys accused of raping two White women on a train in Alabama. Of course, the Scottsboro boys represent just one example among the many stories of Black men who were murdered over false accusations in the name of protecting White women during the Jim Crow era. For example, between 1930 and the early 1970s, southern states executed 405 Black men accused of raping White women (Holden-Smith, 1996). The lynching of Black men—and later the wrongful conviction of Black men by racist juries, referred to as "legal lynchings" (Holden-Smith, 1996)—in the name of protecting White women is a reality that scholars have traced from slavery through Reconstruction and Jim Crow to today, from the Scottsboro boys to Emmett Till to the Central Park Five. Knowing this history means expecting the ending as an inevitability; the trial could not have resolved any way other than Tom's conviction and ultimate death. It also deepens the magnitude of Tom's story by contextualizing it in examples of ongoing, systemic racism.

As we consider Tom's story against the historical examples, however, we see that the novel's ending seems different from those historical examples. Although Tom's situation resembles those of Black men who were accused and then put to death, Tom was killed because he was trying to escape jail.

Framing it in this way puts the responsibility for Tom's death on him, letting the White people who arrested and convicted him—knowing the implications of such decisions—off the hook. It is an indication, once again, of the way dominant racial ideology shapes this and many canonical, White-authored texts on the topic of racism.

Plot

The lens begins with the question, What are the central conflicts in the text? Of course, there are many conflicts that we could explore here, but we have chosen to racialize one of the most central. We actually consulted SparkNotes (2019) to inform this decision, because SparkNotes often functions as a litmus test for dominant, New Critical readings of novels in schools. We want to focus on this conflict in particular in order to illustrate how English teachers and their students might analyze it through a CRT lens. SparkNotes explains:

> To Kill a Mockingbird tells the story of the young narrator's passage from innocence to experience when her father confronts the racist justice system of the rural, Depression-era South. In witnessing the trial of Tom Robinson, a Black man unfairly accused of rape, Scout, the narrator, gains insight into her town, her family, and herself. Several incidents in the novel force Scout to confront her beliefs, most significantly when Tom is convicted despite his clear innocence.

The lens asks, What role does race or racism play in the development of these themes? The novel explores the role race and racism play in Scout's and Jem's loss of innocence. Said another way, the racism Tom faces is represented mostly in terms of how it is perceived and understood by White children.

What does the framing of this conflict reveal about the racial ideology of the text? Focusing a story about racism on its effects on the White characters of the story rather than on the people of color who are experiencing it firsthand points to the influence of a dominant White racial ideology. Exploring racism from White perspectives is not inherently bad; it is important for White people to think about racism in relationship to our own lives. That said, it is also important to see the book for what it is and acknowledge that the story is about White characters and reflects a dominant White racial ideology.

Before moving on, we extend our analysis here to explore one more point related to this relationship between racism and Scout's and Jem's loss of innocence. In the novel, Atticus feels hopeful that Scout and Jem, as innocent children, have not yet learned racism; they have not yet had experiences that have "interfered with their reasoning process" (Lee, 1982/1960, p.

220). They are not, readers are to assume from this statement, racist. Atticus wants to protect them from the racism of Maycomb and, most notably in the book, from the racism of the trial process.

But, once again, the lens asks us to consider, To what extent does the text represent these themes in complex or stereotypical racial terms? This way of thinking about racism—that Scout and Jem experience a loss of innocence as they witness racism in the course of the novel—ignores the ways racism works ideologically to organize everyday life in Maycomb. In other words, Scout and Jem already have learned racism and already take racist ideology for granted. They do not question the segregation of their community, the hierarchy of people in Maycomb, the power dynamic between themselves and Calpurnia as their hired household help, the privilege that comes from being born of "background," the idea that the language they speak at home is considered superior to the language Calpurnia speaks at home, or the idea that the jury and the lynch mob are made up of people considered essentially good. In fact, when Dill is upset about the way Tom is treated on the stand, Scout reassures him that that is just the way things are; there is nothing out of the ordinary going on, saying: "Well, Dill, after all he's just a Negro" (Lee, 1982/1960, p. 199).

Scout and Jem do not question these things because racist ideology shapes the thinking of all of Maycomb. So, are Scout and Jem racist or not racist? Understanding racism as ideological means understanding that no one is exempt from racism—not Atticus, not Scout, and not Jem. They are all implicated, even while they protest the hateful behavior of the Ewells, the lynch mob, the jury, and people who would call Atticus a "nigger lover."

Theme

Although there are many themes in the novel, some of which are unrelated to race and racism, we zero in here on the theme of law and justice. And, of course, race and racism play a central role. Given that one of the main conflicts revolves around the heartbreak of the unjust accusation of Tom Robinson and the impossibility of his getting a fair trial because he is a Black man, there is no question that the novel critiques the racism of the legal system.

At times, however, the book waivers on this theme. Atticus delivers many lectures in which he demonstrates strong faith that the legal system, as an institution, works.

> But there is one way in this country in which all men are created equal—there is one human institution that makes a pauper the equal of a Rockefeller, the stupid man the equal of an Einstein, and the ignorant man the equal of any college president. The institution, gentlemen, is a court. . . . Our courts have their faults, as does any human institution, but in this country our courts are the great levelers, and in our courts all men are created equal. (Lee, 1982/1960, p. 205)

Atticus explains to Jem that the breakdown in the courts occurs due to the prejudices of individual jurors. If more attorneys and jurors approached the situation as Atticus and Jem do, then the legal system would work as intended.

> "If you had been on that jury, son, and eleven other boys like you, Tom would be a free man," said Atticus. "So far, nothing in your life has interfered with your reasoning process. Those are twelve reasonable men in everyday life, Tom's jury, but you saw something come between them and reason. . . . The older you grow, the more you'll see. The one place where a man ought to get a square deal is in a courtroom, be he any color of the rainbow, but people have a way of carrying their resentments right into a jury box." (Lee, 1982/1960, p. 220)

To what extent does the text represent these themes in complex or stereotypical racial terms? What do the themes reveal about the underlying ideology of the text? We argue that the novel sends mixed messages on this theme. At times, the novel points out the racism of the legal system, and at other times it defends the legal system. The theme grapples with the tension between a dominant racial ideology, which says that courts treat everyone equally, and an antiracist one, which says that they clearly do not.

These mixed messages may result, in part, from framing racism as an individual/interpersonal issue. Atticus's speeches—and the underlying racial ideology—locate racism in the hearts and minds of individual men, which dismisses the way racism works more powerfully at the institutional/systemic level. Of course, racism in the legal system is not a matter of individual attitudes: Slavery was a law; defining Black people as 3/5 of a person was a law. Understanding systemic racism means acknowledging that courts are not "great levelers"; rather, racism has been been a purposeful part of the legal system from the very beginning.

Point of View

The story is narrated from the point of view of Scout Finch, a precocious little White girl from Maycomb, Alabama. As a child, as a White child, Scout brings a naïve perspective that makes her a bit of an unreliable narrator, but that also succeeds in emphasizing the taken-for-grantedness of racism in daily life. Given that Scout is 6–8 years old through the course of the story, she is often in a position of making observations that call attention to assumptions in ways that make the underlying racial ideology of Maycomb visible. For example, in Chapter 26, when they study democracy in school, Miss Gates, the teacher, asks, "Does anybody have a definition?" Scout replies, "Equal rights for all, special privileges for none" (Lee, 1982/1960, p. 245). Of course, this scene is funny because a savvy reader knows that this statement is untrue. The hypocrisy of the textbook definition of "democracy" is emphasized when Atticus explains to Scout: "There's something in our

---

COUNTERSTORIES FOR *TO KILL A MOCKINGBIRD*

In Chapter 4, we argued that counterstories are valuable not only for offering perspectives of people of color but also for making the Whiteness of
White-authored, canonical texts more apparent. Some counterstories we
like for *To Kill a Mockingbird* include:

- *Assata: An Autobiography* by Assata Shakur. Shakur, a Black
  Panther, details her experiences of having been framed by the
  police in repeated trials that she saw as set up to find her guilty
  before evidence was even presented to the jury. Students could
  interrogate Assata's consistent spelling of court with a *k*—kourt—
  to signal the ways Black people regularly face a kangaroo court,
  one not meant to follow principles of equity, juxtaposing her bold
  statements about the judicial system with those presented by
  Atticus.
- *Death of Innocence: The Story of the Hate Crime That Changed
  America*, a memoir by Mamie Till-Mobley, Emmett Till's mother,
  describing the murder of her young African American son and her
  subsequent contributions to the civil rights movement.
- *March: Book One* by John Lewis and Andrew Aydin, a graphic
  novel rooted in the life experiences of John Lewis, from his
  childhood in Alabama during the Jim Crow era to his participation
  in the civil rights movement.
- *Monster* by Walter Dean Myers, a young adult novel written
  through three different modes—screenplay, journal entries,
  images—to highlight the different ways each mode depicts the
  experiences of a 16-year-old African American boy as he awaits
  trial for murder.

---

world that makes men lose their heads—they couldn't be fair if they tried. In
our courts, when it's a White man's word against a Black man's, the White
man always wins" (p. 220). Putting the fundamental contradiction between
racism and democracy in terms simple enough for a child to understand has
the effect of making it seem obvious, almost absurd.

But this naïve perspective also leads Atticus to explain racism to Scout
in overly simplified terms, terms that send mixed messages about racism.
For example, perhaps it is Atticus's desire to protect Scout's innocence that
leads him to describe Mr. Cunningham's role in a lynch mob as that of a
good man with a "blindspot." When Jem and Scout ask Atticus why he did
not fight back when Bob Ewell spit in his face and called him a "nigger-
lovin' bastard," Atticus suggests that Bob Ewell needed to vent his frustrations because he had been embarrassed in court (and he did not want Bob

Ewell taking those frustrations out on Mayella). What he did not say was that Bob Ewell was in a rage because Atticus called into question the character of a White man to defend a Black man, something that would have been almost unheard of in the Jim Crow South. In these moments, when Atticus explains racism in simplified terms to protect his children, it has the effect of minimizing or excusing racism.

CRT ANALYSIS OF *ONE CRAZY SUMMER*

In this chapter, we apply the CRT lens to a canonical, White-authored text. In that case, the lens is useful for bringing otherwise invisible racial ideologies into relief. But the lens works equally well with texts by and about people of color, including young adult and pop culture texts, to help English teachers and students engage with key concepts central to a deep understanding of texts. To illustrate, we apply the lens to *One Crazy Summer* by Rita Williams-Garcia in Table 5.2 (following the Conclusion).

CONCLUSION

We anticipate that some English teachers may read our analysis of *To Kill a Mockingbird* and say, "You've ruined the novel!" Or, "You are strangling literature by twisting it through this lens." English teachers might say that we are asking *To Kill a Mockingbird* to be something that it is not. As English teachers and lovers of literature ourselves, we understand those concerns. At the same time, however, we know that *To Kill a Mockingbird* often is considered to be "*the* novel" about racism that students read in secondary English classrooms. Many English teachers want to use this novel to engage students with race and racism in meaningful ways. What we aim to share here is an approach that helps to make the complex and sometimes contradictory messages of the book more visible. We offer this lens as a strategy for approaching this novel and other texts from an antiracist perspective.

Table 5.2. CRT Analysis of *One Crazy Summer*

Literary Elements	Questions for Racializing Literary Elements
Characterization	Delphine, Fern, and Vonetta. Cecile/Nzilla. Their father. Big Ma and Big Pa. The camp leaders, including Crazy Kelvin. Hirohito and the other kids at the community center.
	All of the main characters are characters of color. Their racial identity is named, and it is a central part of their identity. Delphine is a rich, dynamic character. She is smart, responsible, complex, compelling. She has to be more grown-up than most kids because she has a lot of responsibilities taking care of her sisters. She is up to the task. Their mother is incredibly complex. Readers' impressions of Nzilla shift as they change for Delphine, whose opinions stem from Big Ma, who never liked or understood Nzilla, to getting to know her and her story better on their month-long visit to Oakland. The story shows Nzilla as a Black feminist who wants to see her daughter "be eleven"—not only carry "adult" burdens—as a way of showing her love for her daughter. Race intersects with gender throughout the novel. Delphine's mother, as a woman, is judged for leaving her children to go to California. White characters are flat and static, mostly portrayed as perpetuating racism.
	With complex and positive representations of Black women and girls, including those who take an active role in social justice (especially via the Black Panthers), this novel challenges stereotypes.
Setting	Set in Oakland, California. Much of the novel takes place at a Black Panthers camp for youth in their community. It takes place during the civil rights movement. But it also references Big Pa and Big Ma's home in the Deep South and the racism they faced just trying to drive to Alabama.
	The novel racializes setting from the start, beginning from the girls' experience flying to Oakland from New York and attempting to not make themselves a "grand Negro spectacle" by drawing too much attention to themselves for bad behavior. There are also allusions to leaders and artists of color throughout the novel. The girls like to sing pop songs by Black artists and imitate them in their imaginative play. They also learn a lot about the Black Panthers, including about Huey Newton, imprisoned and the leader of the group, but also "Little Bobby"—the innocent child killed by police.
	Rita Williams-Garcia tells a version of history that is not often told, especially in children's and young adult literature. Most students in school learn about Martin Luther King, Jr. If they learn about the Black Panthers at all, they likely learn that they were a militant group. Williams-Garcia's depiction of the Black Panthers as committed to community activism and providing basic services that the community needs, challenges stereotypes about the group.

Literary Elements	Questions for Racializing Literary Elements
Plot	Conflict between Delphine and her sisters and her mother for abandoning them and seemingly not caring about them during this summer visit. The fact that Nzilla is affiliated with the Black Panthers signals that race and racism are also central, overarching conflicts in the story.
	Race plays both a small, pervasive role and a more dramatic role in the overarching plot of the book. Delphine regularly notices the impact of race in her experiences in the world. She notes it when she is being tracked in a store as a Black girl; when a White, foreign family in San Francisco photographs her as an object; and when she notices the poverty—and comfort of being in an all-Black community—in Oakland, versus visiting the more open and exciting—and difficult for them as Black girls—San Francisco. In the larger plot around race and racism in the United States and in Oakland, all of the heroes are Black activists taking charge of their community and aware of how "militant" leaders are getting framed by the police and the government.
	The story is very much told through a Black gaze, rendering visible the ways that Delphine and her sisters learn to take on a more forceful, proud Black identity because of their summer with Nzilla and the Black Panthers. They stop straightening their hair; stop being overly polite in relation to Whites; advocate for Blackness; and speak out on a stage through poetry.
Theme	Social action. There are many examples of social action in the novel: the summer camp itself, activities of the summer camp, the posters, and the community center giving back to the community. Delphine's mother is engaged in social action, and the girls are as well when they take the stage. Fern's role in outing an infiltrator within the Black Panthers is also agentic.
	Black people are active in their own resistance to racism and taking responsibility for social action in their community. The theme is represented in very complex, nuanced ways.
	The theme interrupts the kinds of White savior narratives students often encounter in school literature curriculum.
Point of View	The text was written by Rita Williams-Garcia, and it is told from the point of view of Delphine, the main character.
	Rita Garcia-Williams is a person of color telling a story rooted in her own experiences during the civil rights era. In the field of children's and young adult literature, a long line of scholarship has emphasized the importance of an author's racial identity to contributing to the authenticity of a story. Her author's note at the end of the book further contributes to the authenticity as she shares her family's connections to the Black Panthers.
	This perspective interrupts dominant racial ideology.

CHAPTER 6

Planning for and Responding to Race Talk

Throughout the book, we have explored various ways to initiate and sustain antiracist literature instruction in White spaces. Of course, much of the actual work of antiracist literature instruction gets done through talk, race talk. *Race talk* refers to dialogue that addresses the topics of race, racism, Whiteness, and White privilege (Sue, 2015). One of the central goals of racial literacy is to be able to engage in race talk, even when it is hard and uncomfortable to do so. While many English teachers are on board with initiating conversations about race and racism, many also know that it can present challenges, especially when students resist or subvert our line of questioning or say problematic things. Because race talk can feel emotional, unpredictable, and even explosive, English teachers sometimes feel ill-equipped to handle potential challenges that may arise.

Obear (2017) validates many of the feelings we have heard English teachers express when it comes to engaging in or facilitating race talk, noting that common fears include:

- What if I make a mistake?
- What if I say something stereotypic or biased?
- What if I can't handle a situation?
- If I don't manage this well, people could get hurt.
- Am I making this worse?
- The conversation will get out of control.
- I don't know enough to engage in this conversation effectively.

Perhaps you can relate to feeling any or all of these fears. We certainly can. In our own experiences, we have found that we continually re-commit to engaging our students in race talk not because we have overcome these fears, but despite them. Guided by the above questions and comments, this chapter examines the concept of race talk in an effort to understand not only what we are striving for, but also what makes it difficult. Then, we offer principles of practice we have found valuable for initiating and sustaining race talk in our own classrooms.

COMMON CHALLENGE: MANAGING RACE TALK

Carlin and students in her English methods course had read *To Kill a Mock-ingbird* and were talking about possibilities and challenges of engaging directly with race in the teaching of the novel. They read excerpts of Bonilla-Silva's (2013) work about colorblindness, along with Haviland's (2008) article on White educational discourse, a term we define below. Leading up to this discussion, Carlin and her students collaboratively developed discussion norms for talking about racism. In this excerpt, students were considering whether they should talk about racism with their own future students and why. We decided to share this particular transcript excerpt because it reflects a difficult moment, one that Carlin found professionally challenging and personally triggering.

Troy: I just don't have time to care about whether somebody's Black or White or red, purple, green. It just, it doesn't really, it doesn't matter to me, when I look at someone and say, oh, that's an intelligent human being who can contribute something to my life, my experience, or somebody else's life or experience.

Carlin: Rori?

Rori: I think sometimes when we talk about colorblindness and trying to, like, not see these races, it's impossible to not see color or race, or it's just, like, I can't look at you and be like, huh, you're not wearing glasses. You know, like, we don't, we take it as such a negative thing if you're not blind to color that as soon as you struggle or fail to do that, then it's like, oh, you're automatically a bad person because you're acknowledging something that exists. . . . So I personally don't agree with the concept of colorblindness. That's my personal opinion, because I think it's, I don't wanna say ignorant, but I'm gonna say ignorant.

Carlin: Colorblindness is really complicated. Some people would say that if we would just stop talking about it, if we'd stop categorizing people that way, racism would go away. Or that if we talk about race, it's gonna make it worse.

John: I think, if you don't see color, then you really don't see students. You know what I mean? If you just see your students, you don't see their experiences and what struggles they've gone through, see what you have to be as a teacher to best teach them. If you don't see color, then you don't see anything.

Troy: Like obviously, if you're gonna say that you can't, you can't see the fact that one person is, like, darker skinned or different shaped facial features or something based on their race, like, obviously you're being ignorant. But it's not that, it's not that I don't see color. It's that I don't judge based on it. And that's what, that's what we as a society need to be, like, looking at. . . . But at the same time, if there's things that are, like, patterns, I've heard before from people that stereotypes are stereotypes for a reason. There's people that say that, and like if there's, like, if there's patterns, I think there can be stereotypes that go along with those patterns, but there's almost always, like John said at the beginning of class, there's other contributing factors to stereotypes that people have. Like in this next article that we read, there's a girl that worked at a store and most of the time if they got robbed, it was by an African American, like, person. So an African American person came into the store, there was more of a chance to watch and make sure that things were going to be all right. If it's a statistical, like, fact, if it's a statistical fact, like, I don't know how you cannot have that play into what you think. But that doesn't mean you have to judge people based on it and be negative toward people based on it. You can take that into account.

Carlin: Honestly, we don't know if that's statistically true or not. The quote from the article is a student repeating something she'd heard based on a stereotype and attributing it to a statistic.

Troy: I feel like we're putting it into a binary as in, like, we talk about it or we don't talk about it. I'm pretty much just challenging the way that we address it because I don't feel, like, "let's talk about racism." I don't think that is what kids really, like, need right now. At one point in history, yeah, we needed to address the fact that there's an issue that's going on because it's a highly negative thing, but, like, there's so much like negativity within our culture right now.

What the transcript does not show is that, a few moments later, triggered by Troy's comments and worried about the emotions of other students in the class, Carlin responded to Troy's comments with a long and authoritative explanation full of statistics and examples of systemic racism designed to shut Troy down. Carlin used her position as the authority in the room, along with her own understanding of many examples of systemic racism, to have the final word on the matter. She left the class feeling upset with herself for doing exactly what she had *not* wanted to do—getting emotional and shutting the discussion down.

At one point during the discussion a student walked out, saying that she didn't feel well. Despite following up with this student later, Carlin still does not know whether she left due to this discussion. After class, another student visited Carlin in her office to say that although she felt the discussions they were having in class were valuable and productive, they were making her feel anxious and upset.

WHY THIS MATTERS FROM AN ANTRACIST PERSPECTIVE

Unpacking this scenario in light of what research has to say about race talk may offer insight into challenges that other English teachers face when they initiate discussions about race and racism in their own classrooms.

Race Talk Is Notoriously Difficult

Many White students are not used to talking about race or racism. In fact, when we raise this issue in our classrooms, our White students sometimes tell us that it is the first time that anyone has asked them to consider themselves in racial terms. Moreover, White students are not often conscious of the ways Whiteness shapes their worldview, factors into their identities, or influences their experiences; race talk can be difficult precisely because it makes White people examine that which typically has been very carefully unexamined. Janks (2002) suggests that when schooling attacks students at their core (here, racial) identity level, we might expect to see them "fighting for their lives" (p. 20). Perhaps it is no wonder that when White students are asked to engage directly with the topic of racism, it evokes strong emotions.

Looking at the transcript in this larger context of race talk, Carlin is reminded that Troy's response is not singular; it is predictable, expected. In fact, remembering that race talk is difficult, and remembering that race talk asks White students to examine parts of themselves that they may not have considered before, may offer Carlin some necessary perspective for thinking about Troy's comments differently, without getting heated herself. In fact, Troy's response might have been met with a greater level of understanding of what might have been personally involved for him as a White student examining racism. Our intention here is not to let Troy off the hook for racism, but to think about how to respond to comments like these more productively in the future.

White Talk Is Notoriously Difficult

Facilitating race talk is difficult because White people often subtly and not-so-subtly sabotage discussions about racism. Talking about race and racism violates social norms that encourage White people not to bring those topics up. Talking about racism is not what White people typically have been taught to do, and it is not what we are used to doing in school. Instead, *not* talking about race and racism can seem polite and politic (e.g., Tatum, 2000), while calling attention to those subjects can be perceived as a racist act in and of itself. For all of these reasons, White people have learned to engage in White talk, a range of strategies for avoiding, subverting, and sidestepping race talk, including ways of seeming to talk about race and racism without really being honest or delving into depth (McIntyre, 1997; Trainor, 2005). White talk is characterized by denial, avoidance, defensiveness, and colorblindness. Sue (2015) notes that "maintaining one's innocence by avoiding racial topics is a major strategy used to hold on to one's self-image as a good, moral, and decent human being who is innocent of racial bias and discrimination" (p. 13).

We interpret Troy's initial comment, "I just don't have time to care about whether somebody's Black or White or red, purple, green," as an example of White talk (McIntyre, 1997; Trainor, 2005). On the surface, Troy seems to be arguing against racism to the extent that he claims that race does not really matter to him. Yet, his characterization of "race" as "Black or White or red, purple, green" suggests that our references to specific racial categories are silly and not a legitimate topic for our attention. This is how White talk works: White people shut down discussions of racism while also protecting ourselves from being seen as racist. White talk presents a confounding challenge for teachers because it subverts our efforts to engage directly with the topic of racism. Being able to identify White talk can help English teachers know how to respond strategically in the moment by guiding the discussion back to the topic at hand.

Race Talk Incidents

While White talk can be subtle and evasive, even difficult to notice and detect as it is happening in the moment, another kind of challenge, which we refer to as *race talk incidents*, describes the more overt instances in which students say racist things to which we need to respond. Race talk incidents encompass any school-based incident tied to race that feels risky precisely because it is race-related. Sometimes it involves someone saying something racist; but it also might be a response—walking out of a room—that is tied to the topics of race and racism and invites teacher reflection.

In the excerpt above, Troy claims that it is a "statistical fact" that African Americans are more likely to steal. He quotes an article that Carlin and her students read together in which a White university student is cited as making this claim in a teacher education class (see Haviland, 2008). To be clear, the example he quotes is not a statistical fact; it is an anecdote told by a White teacher candidate in another university classroom, which the researcher characterizes as a problematic example. Troy's comment offended several students in class, and those students expressed their exasperation with having to listen to his racist views. We consider this to be an example of a race talk incident.

Race talk incidents can feel unpredictable, they can catch us off guard, and they can leave us feeling ill-equipped for handling the moment or even regretful for bringing up the topic in the first place. Although it is not surprising that these incidents arise in the classroom, given that students' comments generally reflect dominant thinking about racism in our society, they can be unnerving nonetheless.

And they can feel like failures from the teacher's perspective. In fact, Carlin admits that she felt uncertain about how to handle this situation in the moment, unsure about how and when to shut a Troy's line of thinking down. On one hand, research has shown that teachers are often too quick to shut down discussions about racism, before students have a chance to reach any sort of depth (e.g., Glazier, 2003; Pollock, 2004). Shutting discussions down results in recycling the kind of surface-level talk students are used to in (White) schools. English teachers serious about discussions of racism often encourage students to be open, to ask frank questions. For that to happen, English teachers cannot jump on every student who expresses a problematic viewpoint. On the other hand, if teachers offer students time and space for an open discussion, students may say or do things that will offend, even hurt, others. Although Carlin *did* need to intervene to address Troy's racism in this exchange, she can see now that she had several alternatives for handling that situation more effectively in the moment. We explore those alternatives in the last section of this chapter.

No Matter How Much We Plan, Race Talk Will Be Difficult

One of the arguments of this book has been that English teachers can anticipate and prepare for race talk by front-loading readings and discussions of racial literacy early in the course. For example, we have suggested that teachers could share Bonilla-Silva's (2013) concept of colorblindness, explaining how it often works to protect the speaker from charges of racism. Then, if colorblindness is used in class, teachers and students can work together to call each other out about it. But, in this case, Carlin *did* teach about colorblindness. In the transcript, we see Rori step in and name Troy's comment as colorblindness. In response, Troy changes course, agrees with Rori that colorblindness is ignorant, and tries a different tactic. While we know that deliberate planning is necessary for antiracist literature instruction, we also know that even if we do everything we know how to do to set up for a smooth discussion, we cannot plan our way out of the discomfort that often comes with discussing racism. We cannot avoid the fact that race talk can be—understandably should be—hard and uncomfortable.

WHAT YOU CAN DO: USE PROACTIVE AND REACTIVE STRATEGIES FOR MANAGING RACE TALK

Given the long list of potential challenges, why should we continue to initiate race talk in our classrooms? Our answer to this question is twofold. First, we do it because productive race talk can contribute to racial literacy and racial identity development (Pasque, Chesler, Charbeneau, & Carlson, 2013). Sue (2015) explains:

> It has been shown that honest race talk is one of the most powerful means to dispel stereotypes and biases, to increase racial literacy and critical consciousness about race issues, to decrease fear of differences, to broaden one's horizons, to increase compassion and empathy, to increase appreciation of all colors and cultures, and to enhance a greater sense of belonging and connectedness. (p. xiii)

Second, we commit to race talk because the curriculum and students in our classrooms raise the topics of race and racism regularly, whether we intend to address them or not, and the consequences of *not* engaging with those topics are detrimental for both students of color and White students. Sue (2015) explains that remaining silent on the topics of race and racism can leave students of color feeling unheard or marginalized, experiencing negative effects on their mental health, perceiving classrooms as hostile learning environments, and feeling less able to be productive. For White students, silence around race and racism can perpetuate an inaccurate or limited worldview, interfere with opportunities to develop racial consciousness, and lead to their own sense of shame around their racial identity.

Ideally, we strive to talk about race and racism directly, to create settings in which individuals approach race talk as an opportunity for authentic dialogue, to commit to staying open to and engaged with divergent perspectives, and to knowing that discussions may not end with consensus or answers or even closure. Singleton (2006) describes these opportunities for race talk as "courageous conversations." Courageous conversations succeed in engaging individuals who typically choose to remain silent, sustaining the conversation when it gets uncomfortable or heated, and deepening thinking to the point where authentic understanding occurs. Goals of productive race talk include making the invisible visible; confronting biases, prejudices, and fears; and helping one another understand ourselves as racial/cultural beings (Sue, 2015). In this section, we lay out proactive strategies for preparing for race talk and reactive strategies for responding productively to race talk incidents in predominantly White spaces. We describe each of these strategies in depth and use them to consider the possible ways Carlin might have managed the opening exchange differently.

Proactive Strategies

We have often heard that English teachers should embrace teachable moments when students ask questions or make comments that raise complex issues, including those related to race. Teachers, the message goes, should not worry about having all of the answers when engaging in these discussions with their students, exposing learning as a lifelong endeavor for everyone. On one hand, we can see where this message comes from: Engaging in discussions of race and racism is often better than shutting them down. On the other hand, responding to the teachable moment can sometimes create new problems that teachers may not have or could not have anticipated. In this section, we argue that there are things that teachers can do to plan proactively for race talk.

Commit to Your Own Growth. We list this strategy first, because, as Sue (2015) argues, strategies for facilitating race talk will do little good without a facilitator's racial literacy. In fact, Sue (2015) and his research team found that achieving successful race talk in classrooms depends a lot on the extent to which White teachers have engaged in their own identity work outside of the classroom, the extent to which we feel comfortable and prepared to engage in race talk ourselves, and the extent to which we have had practice engaging in these kinds of discussions with others. Conversely, when teachers feel uncomfortable or underprepared, we are more likely to withdraw from the conversation or shut race talk down when it comes up. Those of us who strive to be antiracist teachers must do the necessary work of confronting our own biases, prejudices, and assumptions if we hope to accomplish that work with our students. We also might look for opportunities to participate in discussion about racism ourselves, outside of the classroom.

Establish Discussion Norms. We recommend preparing for race talk by using the common strategy of establishing discussion norms in collaboration with students (e.g., Singleton, 2006). In our own classes, we begin by asking students, "Have you participated in discussions about race and racism in the past? How did you know if it was going well or not? What are norms that we could agree on to make race talk productive in this class?" We encourage students to be specific and concrete. To illustrate, we say: "Rather than saying 'Be respectful,' please strive to give concrete suggestions like, 'Don't look at your phone or laptop while others are speaking.'" It also can be helpful to offer one or a few sample norms that students in the past have agreed upon to get the ball rolling. Next, we invite students to work in groups of two or three to come up with a few ideas they would like to contribute to the whole group. Our students have come up with norms like:

- Allow for multiple perspectives
- Actively listen with an open mind rather than preparing your argument
- Give people the benefit of the doubt; if they say something problematic, ask clarifying questions before judging
- Use "I" statements to avoid speaking for groups (e.g., "we") because everyone's experience is different

- Use specific terms like "White people" or "people of color" rather than pronouns like "us" and "them"
- Avoid "side eyes" or side talk during discussion
- What happens in our class, stays in our class; within reason, avoid extending someone's vulnerability by sharing the experience insensitively outside of class

Setting up norms always takes longer than we think it is going to take. It can take time to iron out the particular wording of norms to our satisfaction, or it can take time for students to come to consensus if they disagree on norms. We have learned to leave plenty of time for this work, because negotiating the norms for talking *about* race and racism delves into useful topics like power, voice, and oppression—all of which are valuable.

Our students often refer to these norms during whole-group conversations, sometimes requesting that we add new norms to the list to deal with situations as they arise. An added benefit of having the discussion about norms early on in the course has been the implicit message that we intend to have in-depth discussions about race and racism that go beyond the surface level.

Returning to the opening scenario, it is worth mentioning that Carlin and her students had taken time to establish norms. One thing Carlin could have done was to refer to the discussion norms the class agreed on, to point out that she and Troy were monopolizing the air time, and therefore they were not doing a good job of welcoming a variety of perspectives. Carlin might have said, "Let's make sure we are sticking to our norm of ensuring all voices are heard. Let's hear from someone who hasn't had a chance to talk." That simple move might have changed the trajectory of the discussion.

Leverage White Educational Discourse as a Tool. Haviland (2008) digs even more deeply into the notion of White talk, especially as it relates to classrooms, with her concept of White educational discourse. White educational discourse documents specific moves that White people engage in White-dominant educational settings to subvert, avoid, and resist productive race talk, such as:

- ***Avoiding words:*** going to great lengths to avoid race-based terms (e.g., saying ethnic instead of racial)
- ***False starts:*** editing as we talk because we are hesitant to say race-related words (e.g., making several attempts to start a sentence)
- ***Safe self-critique:*** downplaying our own implication in racism (e.g., critiquing our own racism in examples that are safely framed in the past or illustrate that they we no longer think this way)
- ***Asserting ignorance or uncertainty:*** defaulting to "I don't know" as a way of shirking responsibility for particular viewpoints or for participating in race talk

- *Letting others off the hook:* interrupting others' critiques of themselves and racism by affirming that they're not so bad or not racist
- *Citing authority:* citing others for race-based critiques as a way to distance oneself from them
- *Silence:* refusing to engage in or participate in race talk, often accompanied by body language or other nonverbal cues that indicate resistance or discomfort
- *Changing the topic:* shifting the focus of power and oppression away from the topic of race and racism to focus on other forms of oppression or other topics altogether, to distance ourselves from racism
- *Affirming sameness:* emphasizing similarities rather than differences (e.g., critiquing instances of racism by saying they are things "we all do")
- *Joking:* using humor, jokes, and laughter to establish sameness among the group, head off or distance oneself from a critique, or interrupt the flow of dialogue
- *Agreeing and supporting:* "helping" White individuals rather than pushing them to deeper examination of our own racism; used to make everyone feel comfortable and support the status quo
- *Praising and encouraging:* overshadowing challenge and questioning with praise and encouragement
- *Teacher and student caring:* caring, comforting, and seeking consensus—supporting the cohesion of the group and everyone's good feelings—as a way of prioritizing the status quo over challenging racism
- *Socializing and sharing personal information:* divulging personal information as a way to build connection and confidence rather than risk fissures resulting from challenging race talk
- *Focusing on barriers to multicultural education:* emphasizing barriers, including "bad Whites," as obstacles in making progress, rather than examining ourselves and our own implications in racism

We list and define each feature of White educational discourse here because we have found each one of them enormously helpful in our own teaching for understanding why and how race talk often breaks down. When we are able to see these particular moves, we are more likely to be able to redirect toward antiracism in the moment.

Moreover, while White educational discourse has been used as a tool for analyzing the breakdown of race talk in research, we argue for it as a powerful teaching tool in predominantly White spaces. Sophia has had success reading the Haviland (2008) article together with her students to teach them about features of White educational discourse. Then, as a group, Sophia and her students use the terms to reflect on their own race talk in order to call themselves out when they recognize it in discussion. More often, Sophia has seen students use these terms in their reflective writing to evaluate engagement in race talk in classes or even outside of school.

In middle school or high school, we could imagine providing an excerpted list of White educational discourse "moves" or summarizing the article instead of reading it in its entirety. English teachers could give students opportunities to practice identifying White educational discourse together in class by analyzing transcripts featuring race talk. Sophia has found that students easily recognize these moves once they learn the vocabulary.

It is important to acknowledge that some students—and teachers—can feel intimidated at first by the concept of White educational discourse, which can cause them to be overly careful or tongue-tied in race talk discussions. Of course, we do not want to hinder White students or teachers in their efforts; rather, we emphasize our goals for harnessing White educational discourse toward antiracist goals.

Reactive Strategies

No matter how much we plan or prepare, facilitating race talk presents challenges for even the most experienced teachers. What can teachers do in the midst of race talk to keep it on track and keep students engaged? What can we do when challenges arise? Next, we describe strategies teachers can use during discussions about race and racism to respond to common challenges in the moment.

Embrace Discomfort as Growth. Many scholars who write about this topic (e.g., Obear, 2017; Singleton, 2006) remind teachers to expect and embrace discomfort. In fact, Petrone (2015) encourages teachers to help students embrace discomfort as a sign of growth. He argues that one way of helping students to work through feelings of resistance is to introduce them to the concept of cognitive dissonance as it relates to learning. Petrone honors the fact that so much learning, especially critical literacy learning, does not come without some level of discomfort or loss. We suggest applying his recommendation to prepare White students for racial literacy learning as a process of loss, one that can be emotional and uncomfortable. We can acknowledge with students that these feelings make absolute sense given what is at stake and the ways we, as White people, typically learn about race and racism in childhood. In other words, English teachers can set up discomfort as a meaningful part of the experience, rather than something to be avoided or ignored.

In this case, Carlin could have acknowledged the tension in the classroom and turned the focus of the discussion to those feelings as a normal

A Proactive Approach to Discussing the N-Word

Whether the class is studying *Adventures of Huckleberry Finn, To Kill a Mockingbird,* or *Of Mice and Men,* the teacher likely will have to address the N-word with students at some point. English teachers typically are encouraged to discuss the issue with students prior to reading novels that feature the word. But what, exactly, should we say and how can we answer some of students' common questions? Here, we draw heavily on our colleague Justin Grinage's (2013) outstanding work, which offers us a step-by-step guide for teaching about the N-word. While we would recommend his chapter in its entirety, we summarize his approach here.

Step 1: Prepare Self and Students

Grinage begins by establishing discussion norms and agreements for courageous conversations (Singleton, 2006) with his students. He also gives students at least a week's notice to prepare themselves emotionally.

Step 2: Write About the N-Word

Before talking, he asks students to write about discriminatory slurs (nigger, nigga, gay, and retard) with the prompt:

- What are your feelings regarding these words?
- Do you feel it is okay to say any of these words?
- How would you feel about saying any of these words in class?
- Would you be offended if someone read the word or said the word in class discussion or while reading it aloud?
- What additional comments, questions, or concerns do you have?

Step 3: Understand Historical and Modern Usages

Drawing on research from *Nigger: The Strange Career of a Troublesome Word* by Randall Kennedy (2008), Grinage offers his students a presentation of important points in the historical evolution of the word. At this phase, he also shares personal anecdotes about his own and his family's experiences with the word. He encourages White teachers to do the same.

Step 4: Establish Expectations and Discuss the Word

Before discussion finally begins, he emphasizes that at no point does anyone, including the teacher, say the word out loud. Everyone uses the phrase "the N-word." During the discussion, he often relies on the "boiling pot" metaphor to answer students' common questions. The boiling pot metaphor makes clear that in the early 1600s, the water in the pot (around the connotation of the word) was just warm. As the word was used over the years to dehumanize and humiliate Black people, the water began to heat up, to simmer, and then to boil. Now, whenever the word is said, it carries the historical and emotional temperature of White people's gruesome behavior. At any point, the water, which is already hot, can boil over or explode.

A PROACTIVE APPROACH TO DISCUSSING THE N-WORD, CONTINUED

Step 5: Reflect and Debrief

Grinage asks his students to revisit their initial writings to see whether their views have changed at all as a result of their discussions.

Teachers might complement their use of Grinage's suggestions with those offered by Koritha Mitchell (2019) in her podcast, where she reinforces many of Grinage's suggestions and offers some variations, too. The work of scholars of color like Grinage and Mitchell have offered us, as White teachers, tremendous insight and support for engaging in this work.

---

and expected part of antiracist teaching and learning by saying, "I am noticing that I am feeling emotional in response to this discussion, and I wonder if others are too." Then, "Why is it that talking about racism raises these feelings for us? How might we think about these feelings as a positive sign that we are doing something worthwhile?"

Know Your Own Trigger Responses. Students are not the only ones who have emotional reactions during race talk. Teachers, too, can expect to be triggered at times. It may be comforting to expect this possibility and prepare for it, knowing that it is a common experience for many teachers. Obear (2017) suggests that it can be helpful for teachers to identify how they typically respond during triggering situations. She characterizes reactions in terms of "fight, flight, freeze, or flounder" responses. Those who are inclined to "fight" may find themselves arguing and debating, raising their voices, trying to silence others, dismissing or minimizing others' comments, making sarcastic or off-hand remarks, turning others' words against them, or criticizing or shaming others. Those who are inclined toward a "flight" response may get defensive, become guarded, ignore or avoid issues, minimize or downplay the issue or conflict, shut down, disengage, or use humor. Those who "freeze" during these times may zone out, feel overly anxious and scared, or forget what they intended to say or do. Those who "flounder" may give contradictory comments/examples, continue talking even though they feel "out of body," or go off on a tangent. People may display different aspects of each of these at different times.

Carlin demonstrated a fight response in her effort to shut Troy down. Although she knows that this is not an effective way to respond, she has found great comfort in learning that these responses are normal. Since then, being able to identify these trigger responses in herself in the moment has helped her to be able to slow down and rethink how she can manage a difficult situation as it is occurring. In fact, this one realization has been a game changer for Carlin in terms of offering the personal awareness necessary for taking the discussion in a different, more productive direction. Obear's categories could be used proactively as well. Teachers could ask students to write about a race talk incident that triggered them, and then use these categories to help students gain some understanding about how they typically react. That awareness could be useful in future race discussions.

Expect Racist Comments. Thinking proactively, teachers working in White-dominant contexts can presume that there will be students in the room who hold racist assumptions and that these views likely will enter the room. This presumption could be shared with the class when setting up for race talk. To help, teachers could show a clip of Robin DiAngelo (2018), expert on Whiteness and race talk, discussing the *likelihood* that Whites hold racist views in a highly racialized and racist society like the United States. In "Why 'I'm Not Racist' Is Only Half the Story," DiAngelo discusses "the inevitable absorption of a racist worldview" by White people as the assumption from which race talk could *begin*. That will help to alleviate the worry that students in the class will be exposed as racist, since that is already presumed.

Sophia has used this opening (sans the clip since she did not yet have access to it) to indicate her own focus in the class as they launched antiracist work: "I am not going to be sitting in discussions, listening, ready to pounce at someone when they utter something racist as evidence of their racism. I already assume you are racist; as am I, and I am the parent of two children of color. It is the air we breathe. Our efforts here are to work together to help each other take note of our racism, acknowledge it, show it to the air in order to begin the laborious and necessary work of dispelling it." In their reflective writing, especially, Sophia's students comment on the shock of this opener and the relief of someone acknowledging what usually is unacknowledged in White spaces.

Acknowledge Inappropriate Remarks. Many English teachers have expressed to us that they do not know what to do when a student makes a racist comment. We can validate that anxiety. Confronting racism can feel risky, because being perceived as racist reflects many White people's greatest fears at moments like these. That said, it is important for all students— White students and students of color—that the racist comment is acknowledged and addressed. Obear (2017) gives us concrete moves for responding in these moments. First, she suggests confirming what you heard with a response such as, "I thought I heard you say_____. Am I right?" If the student disagrees with your version, she explains, you may decide to end the conversation, assuming that you misunderstood and giving the speaker an opportunity to disown the comment gracefully. If the student acknowledges making the comment, she suggests exploring the intent behind the comment with a response like, "Help me understand what you meant by that," or

"What were you hoping to communicate with that comment?" Another option is to explore the impact of the comment by asking, "What impact do think that comment could have?" or "What message do you think that comment sends?" Teachers can share their perspective of the probable impact of these types of comments by saying something like, "Many people would take that comment to mean . . . " or "That comment only perpetuates negative stereotypes and assumptions. . . . " Finally, if the student persists, a teacher has a right and responsibility to ask the student to stop making such comments, doing so either one-on-one or in front of the class, depending on the norms and practices of the room. In some ways, this technique validates Carlin's decision to interrupt Troy's line of thinking in the moment—although, as our examples in this section show, she likely had many different options for going about it.

Use PAIRS to Navigate Difficult Moments. This strategy builds on the previous one. Sue (2015) argues that responding to the content of the conversation may not be as effective as responding to the feelings evoked by the conversation. Likewise, Obear (2017) offers PAIRS as a collection of skills that teachers can use to respond in these moments. The acronym stands for:

P: PAN the environment and yourself; describe what you notice or engage others based on what you see. Some questions or sentence stems that can be useful include:

- I'm noticing that I'm feeling . . . ; anyone else?
- I noticed how quiet everyone got; I'm wondering what is going on for folks.
- It seems some people were impacted by that statement, am I right?
- I'm noticing that you're speaking with a lot of energy and emotion . . .
- I'm noticing that people get interrupted as they try to share . . .

A: ASK about the specifics behind the person's comment or behavior

- Could you say more about that . . . ?
- Can you give us an example of what you're saying?
- Help me understand what you mean by that.

I: INTERRUPT the dynamics

- Let's slow down the conversation and talk about what just happened . . .
- I'm going to interrupt and try a different approach to this conversation . . .
- We are not engaging according to our group norms . . .
- Let's take a breath . . .

R: RELATE to the person or the comment/behavior

- I relate to what you're saying; I have felt the same way . . .
- How do others relate to that comment?
- What you're saying seems to relate to what so-and-so said . . .

S: SHARE about yourself/self-disclose with a story or an example; your feelings in the moment; the impact of a comment or behavior

- When I hear you say that, I think/feel . . .
- I was socialized to believe that . . .
- I'm beginning to feel . . .
- My heart aches as you tell that story . . .
- I notice I'm feeling a little triggered . . .

We want to acknowledge that some of the PAIRS strategy steps involve relying on White educational discourse moves (e.g., affirming sameness through relating), but do so to promote more productive race talk.

Taking this advice, Carlin could have used the PAN technique and said something like, "I am noticing that I am feeling a little triggered right now. I wonder if others would like to comment on their emotional responses to this discussion." Or, she could have combined the PAN and the RELATE techniques and shared the observation that "I am noticing that you are having an emotional response to this conversation. I am noticing that I, too, am feeling an emotional response to this conversation. Can we talk about that for a moment?"

Facilitate Turn-Taking to Ensure That Marginalized Voices Are Heard.
At times, race talk can begin to reflect power imbalances that favor the dominant racial perspective in the classroom. For example, during a whole-group discussion, students with relative power and privilege may dominate time and space in ways that further marginalize disenfranchised students. In these instances, teachers can facilitate turn-taking to make sure that there is ample space for students whose perspectives most need to be heard at that moment—rather than calling on the first hand up (e.g., Fisher & Petryk, 2017).

Referring to the opening scenario, Troy not only made offensive comments but also dominated air time. As we mentioned above, Carlin could have returned to the norms or facilitated turn-taking in a way that diffused the situation and introduced a wider variety of viewpoints. She might have said, "Let's hear from some others who have not yet had a chance to speak." Or, "Troy, it seems that you and I are taking up a lot of the air time here; let's invite some others to weigh in on the issue."

"MY FRIEND IS RACIST"

A White teacher is reading *To Kill a Mockingbird* and teaching about race and racism with her English 10 honors class, which is majority-White with one student of color, Peter. Peter is in a small group with his good friend, Rebecca. On three separate occasions, while the students were doing groupwork that required discussion, Peter reported to the teacher that Rebecca was racist. In each instance, Peter recapped the discussion that led to this claim, and both the teacher and Rebecca perceived Peter to be joking based on his tone and demeanor. Additionally, when he explained what he saw as racist, the teacher and Rebecca understood that Rebecca's comment was race-related but not racist. The last time this happened, Rebecca said she felt like Peter was always picking on her through these unfair comments. The teacher redirected the conversation back to the classwork.

What can we make of Peter's comments? We interpret Peter as using the phrase "that's racist" to call attention to something race-related that may or may not actually be racist. Given the context, we assume that Peter may be using the safety of the small-group context, his friendship with this White girl, and his joking tone to safely voice his discomfort as the sole student of color in this space during a lesson focused on racism. It is possible that he would not feel safe calling attention to the discomfort of the racial dynamics of the classroom with the White teacher or in the whole group.

We encourage the teacher to not ignore Peter's comment, even if the teacher initially does not understand its cause or trust its "veracity," but to respond in the moment or soon after. When a student of color is telling a White student that she is racist, we should listen to the student of color in an effort to understand what might be going on for that student that we, especially as White teachers, might not realize. Of course, it is not fair for the student of color in the room to have to bear the responsibility of having to say something. However, if students of color do express concern, we need to listen.

To proceed, the teacher might begin with the PAIRS technique of asking Peter for more information. On some level, this White teacher was confused by Peter's use of the term "racist." But, given his repeated comments, she might have asked, "Can you tell me more about what you might mean by that?" If Peter was using that comment to refer to something race-related but not racist per se, then the teacher could have discussed the issue further with the class or the small group, trying as best as possible not to bring too much attention to Peter. The teacher could remind the class that conversations about race in White contexts around literature are rare, making them uncomfortable for those involved, perhaps especially for people of color, but also potentially for White people, like Rebecca.

"MY FRIEND IS RACIST," CONTINUED

We recommend that this conversation, too, be front-loaded as one that might be helpful for establishing a context for such discussions, and one that would be more comfortable if held in *advance* of such incidents rather in reaction to them. Students of color in Sophia's recent White-dominant classes have explained that they sometimes feel as though White students' surprise, guilt, or frustration around the topic of racism is the "fault" of students of color. Such a dynamic is especially troubling given that the purpose of focusing on race in schools is to remedy, not exacerbate, the effects of racism. Still, if something like this takes place in our classes, it makes sense for the entire class to understand it better in the context of race talk dynamics in White spaces (cf. Reyes, 2011).

Take a Meta-Moment. As a new English teacher in a rural, predominantly White, and conservative district in Montana, Horner (2019) writes about her commitment to teaching for racial literacy through literature. That goal presented myriad challenges for her. At times, her White students seemed to resist race talk during their study of *Americanah*. Yet, she worked hard to rethink what she initially saw as "resistance" and to see it as the understandable emotional difficulty of processing new information that challenges students fundamentally. In response, she developed "meta-moments," a term she uses to describe a "time out" during which she and her students step back from the current discussion to take their temperature, reflect on their own feelings, and try to understand the root of those feelings. Horner asks her students to write or talk about two things: (1) How am I feeling? To what can I trace these emotions? and (2) What are we actually talking about when we talk about [the topic that triggered the tension]? She often asks them to do this reflection in writing, which not only gives them an opportunity to slow down and gather their thoughts but also gives her the opportunity to respond to students individually in writing.

This technique might have given Carlin and her students a moment to process their thinking before proceeding with the discussion. Paired with the possibility of "expecting discomfort," Carlin might have taken this opportunity to say not only, "How might we think about these feelings as signs of growth?" but also, "Let's take a moment to process what is happening for each of us at this moment," using Horner's questions above.

CONCLUSION

We can attest that race talk often does not feel good in the moment—and yet we remain convinced of the absolute necessity of it. It is worth noting, for example, that in their final interviews after Carlin's class ended, nearly all of the participants indicated that this discussion and others like it—including Troy's comments and the emotions they caused—illustrated to them just how necessary antiracist literature instruction would be for them as English teachers in their future classrooms, perhaps especially with White students.

CHAPTER 7

Designing Assignments to Build Racial Literacy

Throughout the book, we have emphasized the importance of understanding foundational race concepts, arguing that much about race and racism are facts about which teachers can teach and students can learn—not just individual opinions. At the same time, however, we also must emphasize that race and racism are *more* than curricular topics and concepts. Becoming racially literate also means being able to reflect critically on one's own identity in racial terms. White students must engage in identity work to understand the ways they are constructed racially and the ways race and racial privilege influence their experiences, identities, and worldviews. In this chapter, we turn our attention to how English teachers might design assignments to build students' racial literacy and develop students' racial identities.

COMMON CHALLENGE:
QUESTIONING WHITE RACIAL ASSUMPTIONS

Miranda was in her second English course with Sophia during her senior year. The introductory unit of the course focused on antiracist literature instruction featuring *To Kill a Mockingbird*. Students read articles on key race topics, such as systemic racism, Whiteness, and colorblindness, and applied those concepts to a critical race analysis of the novel.

Coming into the class, Miranda felt that having attended a racially diverse high school meant that she knew more about race than people who had attended less racially diverse schools: "In my high school there was a lot of mixed races—I feel heavily on the Hispanic race. I felt like I knew everything there was to know about how they acted and stuff that went on." In her view at the time, knowledge about race involved knowing how people of color—Latinx people, in her case—acted.

As the course asked Miranda to delve more deeply into racism and Whiteness and introduced her to new race-related concepts, it caused her to rethink some aspects of her own racial identity. For example, Miranda told Sophia in an interview that she quickly realized how little she understood about race and racism by listening to her peers discuss it in online exchanges with Carlin's students and in class discussion:

> Like I said before, coming into the class, I felt like I was more knowledgeable than folks who came from a predominantly White high school. Coming into the class and even starting with *To Kill a Mockingbird* and reading that book through the lens of race, I feel like I was knocked down so many levels, and I have just so much more for me to learn and know and be more aware of. . . . I felt like I was a little more hesitant to talk, and I really didn't participate in any conversations. I still feel like sometimes the word choice can make or break an argument. So I was more hesitant to talk because I wanted to hear other people, their opinions.

Much can be said about what she means by "the word choice" in "mak[ing] or break[ing] an argument," but at least part of that involves how confidently she felt she could contribute to discussions of race based on her existing racial literacy.

WHY THIS MATTERS FROM AN ANTIRACIST PERSPECTIVE

The term *White racial identity* often is used to refer to the extent to which individuals are aware of themselves in racialized terms. As White people begin to grasp complex race concepts, we often begin to "see" or "understand" Whiteness, sometimes for the first time. In other words, White people operate with differing levels of race consciousness, and we begin to develop that consciousness as the inner workings of racism and Whiteness are made more apparent (Frankenberg, 1993). We can see in Miranda's comments that, as Sophia's course introduced her to new race concepts, Miranda began a process of rethinking some of what she thought she knew. This sort of identity work is imperative for building one's racial literacy.

These deliberate efforts to develop racial consciousness, which often include reflecting on one's own beliefs, assumptions, and privileges, can lead to feelings of guilt, shame, or sense of being overwhelmed (Thandeka, 1999). Miranda expressed to Sophia that she felt knocked down so many levels, that she had so much to learn, that she felt hesitant to talk in front of her peers in class. It is important to note that many students have even more dramatic emotional responses than Miranda to antiracist work. Although these are expected reactions to developing racial consciousness, it is also important that White students not remain in a state of guilt or shame, but stay engaged despite discomfort to develop a healthier, more productive identity as an ally or accomplice (Matias, 2016).

While a certain level of discomfort is necessary—and we do not want to completely eliminate the cognitive dissonance needed for racial identity growth—those of us committed to antiracist pedagogy are always working to develop more effective approaches for engaging White students in this work. Lensmire et al. (2013) note that antiracist pedagogies that *begin* with personal examinations of White privilege often raise students' defenses and do little to help White students grasp the idea of racism as systemic. Perhaps, Lensmire et al. and others (Leonardo, 2004; Lowenstein, 2009) argue, White privilege is not the most effective pedagogical starting point. Miranda's example illustrates that building a foundational understanding of complex race concepts can be a useful place to start. When we start with foundational race concepts, new understandings often cause students to reflect on their White racial identity in new ways—often with less resistance than if we started with explorations of White privilege. In fact, many of our White students express gratitude for learning about race and racism, realizing what they have been ignorant of until now.

WHAT YOU CAN DO:
DESIGN ASSIGNMENTS TO SCAFFOLD RACIAL LITERACY

In Chapter 2, we argued for the importance of articulating racial literacy objectives and designing summative assessments to match those objectives using the principle of backward design (Wiggins & McTighe, 2005). In this section, we return to that principle, emphasizing the importance of designing formative assessments to scaffolding students toward our expressed racial literacy goals. Below we lay out pedagogical principles for guiding the design of formative assessments for racial literacy learning. In the next section, we describe two assignments—a collaborative glossary and an exploratory essay—that we have used in our own courses for these purposes.

Principle 1: Begin by Teaching Complex Race Concepts

We recommend that English teachers begin the work of bolstering students' racial literacy by helping students name and define race concepts like systemic racism, colorblindness, and White talk, for example. Next, we suggest that English teachers offer students multiple, low-stakes opportunities to apply their growing understanding to the analysis of literary texts and other race-related scenarios. From there, building on time and practice, English teachers can move on to asking students to apply those same concepts to experiences from their own lives. As we described above, we have seen a reciprocal relationship between developing understanding of foundational race concepts and engaging in White racial identity work.

Principle 2: Use Formative Assessments to Scaffold Racial Identity Work

An important aspect to understand about White racial identity is that individuals do not move along a linear path from ignorance to awareness (cf., Helms, 1990). As E. Johnson (2013) argues, Whites are *always becoming*, continually struggling to recognize and understand the implications of Whiteness and White privilege. In other words, White racial identity work is never "done." A commitment to antiracism constitutes a lifelong journey, one without guarantees of achieving the status of a "good White" once and for all (Thompson, 2003).

Low-stakes, recursive formative assignments can be ideal for scaffolding students' White racial identity work with practice and over time. These formative assessments provide opportunities for students to try on their developing understanding of complex race concepts and can be used to help students work through the shame, guilt, and confusion that often go along with racial identity work. While whole-group discussion certainly can be considered to be a formative assessment, and while much racial literacy learning typically happens through whole-group discussion, we also like to design writing assignments that provide students time to develop, refine, and revise their thinking.

While most writing that students produce in school reflects a discourse of certainty, racial identity work also must include engagements foregrounding *un*certainty, questions, and *slow* realizations. Thompson (2003) argues that when it comes to race consciousness as a White person, "knowing the right answers in advance confines morality and politics to a narrow place" (p. 23). The process of developing understanding of race concepts and racial identity cannot settle into a content sense of achievement, rightness, or superior morality. Rather, we must "trouble the expectation that we can know exactly what will count as antiracist in every situation and thus can always act blamelessly" (p. 23). The best that we can hope for is a tentativeness to our efforts, knowing that it is one dip into the water, one attempt to understand something—something big or small—in our work toward growing racial literacy.

IN THE CLASSROOM:
USING COLLABORATIVE GLOSSARIES AND EXPLORATORY ESSAYS

Collaborative Glossary

Born from the problem illustrated by Miranda, a White student who *desired* but did not yet *exhibit* racial literacy, this assignment is designed to contribute to students' understanding of complex race concepts, by asking them to create a collaborative glossary around race-related terms. A collaborative glossary defines key racial literacy concepts in complex ways, draws on shared readings that utilize and define such terms, and illuminates the meaning and uses of the terms by applying them to a real-world example. Following typical conventions of the genre of a glossary, students define a key term for an audience unfamiliar with it, doing so by relying on shared readings. Students include in-text citations to bolster their definition. If the term is utilized or defined in more than one source, students draw from those sources, making sure to point out any differences in meanings across sources. Students address the significance of the term, explaining why it matters and to whom. The entry is followed with a bibliographic citation.

The collaborative nature of the assignment works in multiple ways. First, the whole group reads a collection of the same "seed texts" (Savini, 2011)—texts central to a topic or argument in a field—so that everyone is working with shared, emerging knowledge around the topic. Additionally, the whole group collaborates in naming and distilling the most significant terms from the readings and in helping to hone one another's explanations via peer feedback. Specifically, the class works through the following steps:

1. Students read two or three key articles about racism, writing about them and discussing them to better ensure shared understandings.
2. The class generates a master list of key terms utilized in the articles, terms that deepen race understandings.
3. Students collaboratively distill the list to one that is most essential and with maximum applicability to them in literary study and in the real world.
4. After being assigned one key racial concept each, students craft a glossary entry that follows glossary genre traits (e.g., opening with an overarching categorization of the term; concise and detailed language; aimed at an audience unfamiliar with the term).
5. Students complement this traditional entry by including a multimodal explanation of how they see the term in action in the real world (i.e., locating an example of the term in use in popular culture and showing why it is an example of the term).
6. Students offer peer feedback on drafts, drawing from their own emerging understandings of a range of racial literacy concepts. We offer feedback on accuracy, thoroughness, flow, and clarity.
7. The final glossaries are posted to a shared site (e.g., class website, Blackboard, etc.) for classmates to utilize in subsequent assignments.

To illustrate, we share an example from one of Sophia's recent courses. The class read three texts from which they distilled key racial literacy concepts: Borsheim-Black's "'It's Pretty Much White'" (2015); Haviland's "'Things Get Glossed Over'" (2008); and a chapter ("The Central Frames of Color-blind Racism") from Bonilla-Silva's *Racism Without Racists* (2013). After they discussed each of these readings independently, students were assigned one text each to mine for concepts to suggest to the class. At this point, teachers ought to accept all terms suggested by students, even though you will likely have more terms than students to define them. Broadcast them on the board for the class to see, so students can work together to distill the list. This distillation process is key to understanding the concepts, to figuring out which are more important and have broader application than others. Next, the class works to trim the list so there is one word for each student. In Sophia's class, the master list included the following key racial literacy terms:

- Whiteness
- White educational discourse
- Naturalization
- Minimization
- Abstract liberalism
- Cultural racism
- Institutional racism
- Societal racism
- Individual racism
- Epistemological racism
- Colorblindness or colorblind racism
- Antiracist pedagogy

After the class agrees on the final list, English teachers can randomly distribute the terms to students. Students then have time to craft their glossary entry and multimodal application draft for peer review. To help them with this writing, we recommend a bit of a genre analysis of glossary entries. Invite students to read two or three examples of glossary entries, analyzing them for key traits. Share these traits on the board and have students take notes to keep alongside them while drafting. During peer review, encourage students to help one another by recommending key quotations or claims from the readings to use as support or, more often, suggesting revisions for readers unfamiliar with the term. Students then revise and refine their drafts.

The following collaborative glossary entry and multimodal illustration in Figure 7.1 were composed in Sophia's recent course by an undergraduate English student, Christine Luongo.

Figure 7.1. Student Glossary Entry for Naturalization

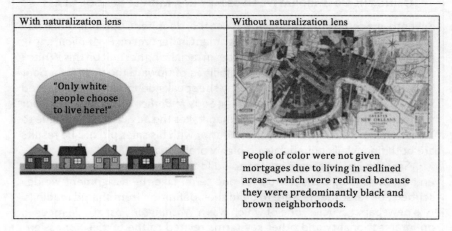

With naturalization lens	Without naturalization lens
"Only white people choose to live here!"	People of color were not given mortgages due to living in redlined areas—which were redlined because they were predominantly black and brown neighborhoods.

Naturalization

Naturalization is one of Bonilla-Silva's four central frames of color-blind racism. It is a "frame that allows whites to explain away racial phenomena by suggesting they are natural occurrences" (Bonilla-Silva, 2013, p. 28). In other words, naturalization is the way that people—primarily white people—say that something is natural rather than racially motivated. For example, when white people say that self-segregation—the process by which people choose to live near or spend time with only people of their own race—is natural—and therefore not racist—because both white and black people do it, they are using the naturalization frame. Naturalization as a frame works to hide the fact that segregation is created through a social process. It seeks to "normalize events or actions that could otherwise be interpreted as racially motivated" (p. 37). Naturalization is often used to justify racial segregation in neighborhoods. People using the naturalization frame will say that it is natural that people choose to live around others of their same race. They claim that this naturalness means that when white people overlook neighborhoods primarily populated by people of color, they are not racist. This frame hides the true primary cause of segregation in housing: redlining. As this NPR video explains ("Why Are Cities So Segregated?"), redlining is the practice that began in the 1930s that marked neighborhoods primarily populated by black and brown people as "hazardous" to give loans to. Wealth is primarily accumulated through property, so black and brown people living in these redlined neighborhoods were not able to build wealth in the

USING THE COLLABORATIVE GLOSSARY IN A MIDDLE SCHOOL CLASS

Seventh-grade English language arts teacher Jennifer Cupp utilized a version of the collaborative glossary assignment in her unit on *Pygmalion*, a 1913 play by George Bernard Shaw. Interested in racializing her unit on this White-authored play that features the possibilities of upward mobility for a poor Victorian woman who changes the way she speaks, Jennifer complemented the play with scenes from the 2018 film, *Sorry to Bother You*. In the film, poor telemarketer Cassius Green, a Black man, takes the advice of a colleague to Whiten his voice in order to succeed better with his sales pitch. The results are both financially beneficial and highly problematic.

Seventh-graders were invited to build their conceptual literacy for the unit by writing a glossary entry for one term. Like the assignment we described above, students were to build their definition from shared readings: two newspaper articles, one of which was a *Washington Post* article focused on intersectionality and other key terms related to the text. Their assignment was collaborative as well, although in a slightly different way than we describe. Students shared their entry with three to four other 7th-graders, from one of the other four 7th-grade classes, who were assigned the same term. As an incentive, the student with the best entry would win a prize from the teachers involved.

The summative assignment for the unit asked students to take a stance on code switching—the practice of changing the way one writes or speaks to adjust to the needs or expectations of an audience, purpose, or genre. The practice of code switching has class and racial implications since the most standardized versions of language tend to be White and middle class (Greenfield, 2011). A formative assignment, meant to encourage students to focus on these issues when watching the end of the film, asked them to consider the film's stance on code switching. In the following excerpt from one student's work, the student uses her own glossary term, *intersectionality*, which she did not need to do, to discuss both the film and the play.

> In the middle of both [texts], Cassius and Eliza are given an opportunity to preform [sic] code switching to become successful. Cassius preforms [sic] code switching and has an opportunity to become a power caller, while, Eliza preforms [sic] and becomes a lady and has the opportunity to open her own flower shop. Lastly, the way Eliza and Cassius get treated, are similar. This is because both of them have to go through Intersectionality [sic] because Cassius is colored and in the lower class, yet is a male. Similar to Eliza, in [sic] where she is treated unfairly because she is a female and in the lower class.

> ### USING THE COLLABORATIVE GLOSSARY IN A MIDDLE SCHOOL CLASS, CONTINUED
>
> In this excerpt, we notice a few ways that her literacy—including racial literacy—has been affected. First, she is able to identify and explain examples of *intersectionality* in the film and the play: the interplay of race and class for Cassius, and gender and class for Eliza. Second, the student also draws on her emerging understandings of the term *code switching* to help her unpack what she noticed in the film, also making connections to the play. As with students in our own college courses, the learning from the glossary entries transfers, migrating to other sites where students now notice it can be applied.

same way that white people living in white neighborhoods—marked as safe areas to offer affordable mortgages—were able to. This inequity of access to wealth building led to people of color staying in these poorer neighborhoods. These effects are still present today, despite the fact that redlining was outlawed in 1968. Therefore, racial segregation between neighborhoods is not merely an issue of self-segregation, as people using the naturalization frame want to believe. Rather, it is a result of the racist practice of redlining.

Christine's entry relies on understanding a key chapter by Bonilla-Silva focused on how White people who do not see themselves as racist utilize one of four "frames" of colorblindness, like naturalization, to explain race-based practices. The requirement to apply the concept to the world requires students to begin to look around them to see the explanation of racism in action. This facet of the assignment begins the process of not only learning a term within a hermetically sealed classroom, but being able to identify it in the world. More subtly, as glossary entry authors, students are effectively working to *persuade* their audience, through writing, to understand racism in more complex ways.

Having employed the collaborative glossary for a few semesters, we have noticed two significant effects that contribute to the way this assignment helps to build racial literacy. First, as long as a glossary entry includes *correct* information about the race concept, whether the entry conforms to the *genre* traits precisely does not seem to affect the student's understanding of the term. In other words, even for glossary entries that might receive lower scores for alignment with genre traits (e.g., conciseness), the mere *attempt* at this genre writing through the suggested process seems to deepen students' long-term understanding of the term to the point that it becomes integrated into their racial understanding.

The second finding we have noticed is that the effects of this glossary work exceed the bounds of the assignment. Well after the glossary has been turned in, we find evidence of its impact in later student work. In other words, students return to their term—or those of peers—to explain other race-based experiences in their lives, in the world. With classroom teachers beginning to utilize this assignment, this finding has been confirmed even further. As we shared above, a 7th-grader who defined the term *intersectionality* also reached for a term defined by a peer—*code switching*—to help her explain the connection between a 2018 film, *Sorry to Bother You*, and a 1913 play, *Pygmalion*, in racialized terms.

Exploratory Essay

The second key assessment that we rely on to deepen students' racial literacy and racial identity development is the exploratory essay. The exploratory essay genre differs from other essays in that it is organized as *thesis-seeking* rather than *thesis-supporting*. This different orientation means that the writing is organized more around *questions* that the writer genuinely pursues than around *claims* for which the writer rallies evidence as support. Writers are expected to "choose a question, problem, or issue that truly perplexes [them]" (Ramage, Bean, & Johnson, 2009, p. 180) and to "keep a problem alive" (p. 177) by "resist[ing] closure" (p. 177) or easy resolutions. The overall effect is the study of a deep question, wherever it takes the student. The form of the essay is narrative; students are telling their own stories of their process.

In this assignment, writers craft multiple drafts of an exploratory essay in which they use a critical race lens to thoughtfully address (1) a piece of literature, (2) their own complex racial identity, and (3) the discussion of at least one race-based incident. The order in which they do this work is up to the writers, as is the way they elect to connect one section of the essay to the rest. Below, we say more about each of the three facets of this task.

Critical Race Analysis of Literature. We ask students to apply a CRT lens (see Chapter 5) to literature to give them practice with potentially new race concepts, to understand the relevance of race and racism to the subject matter they teach, and to get a sense of the depth that is possible in literary analysis when we take the time to teach about key race concepts. Here, Katherine applies her growing understanding of race and racism to her experiences reading *To Kill a Mockingbird* in high school.

> How do you un-love a character that you have loved for years? I fell in love with Atticus Finch when I first read *To Kill a Mockingbird*. . . . My absolute favorite teacher ever loved the book so much and she hoped we would fall in love with Atticus like she had. Atticus and Boo were

heroes, Scout and Jem were so innocent, but Tom Robinson was just a poor victim who was treated unfairly because that's the way it was back then. My teacher is someone who [sic] I considered progressive and opened my eyes to some issues of race in our unit on *To Kill a Mockingbird*. I remember she brought in a podcast reporting on the shooting of Trayvon Martin to show us that racism was still an issue. But adoring Atticus as a hero while addressing racism of 2012 sent mixed signals—ones that I am only now able to unpack.

Over the last week or two I've thought on occasion that it is sad that I don't get to teach it the way my favorite teacher did—I can't be excited to see the kids adore Atticus, but then I catch myself. If I'm sad about that, then that means I am picturing a classroom full of White students like my own high school, and it means I want them to ignore the fact that Atticus is racist. I can't ignore that. As Haviland describes in her article "'Things Get Glossed Over,'" Whiteness can be both "powerful and power-evasive" when White people employ a number of different White educational discourse moves including avoiding words. Avoiding calling out Atticus as a *racist* protects Whites from seeing faults in White characters while also avoiding acknowledging the power he and other White people in the jury and in the community of Maycomb have over their Black community members.

We want to note the way that Katherine used White educational discourse, a concept from her own glossary entry, to explain ways White readers avoid seeing how Whiteness functions in *To Kill a Mockingbird* and how that ultimately perpetuates racism. Through doing so, Katherine also begins to point to rich ways to teach *To Kill a Mockingbird* by emphasizing the role of race in ways that her own schooling did not, but that she is just now beginning to recognize.

Reflection on Individual Racial Identity. We also ask students to apply their evolving racial literacy to reflections on their own lives. For example, throughout her consideration of *To Kill a Mockingbird* above, Katherine is thinking about her own experiences with the novel. Later in the essay, she comments on the ways White people often avoid this sort of reflection.

I am also starting to see how avoiding implication of White characters in literature also means that we are not looking for implication in ourselves (speaking for me and other White people). The same goes for *Huck Finn* as well: when we avoid pointing out the flaws and implicating White characters for their racism, then we avoid doing the same in ourselves. White people will identify with White characters, and so by propping up Atticus as Tom's hero and propping up Huck as a brave, young hero who makes a sacrifice to go to hell to save

Jim, White people can read this literature just to help them feel good about themselves. And so realizing this makes me question my initial reading and love for *To Kill a Mockingbird*. This feeling that I have in these realizations is very uncomfortable. And that is because I have been implicated. I loved reading about Atticus standing up for what I agreed was right too. I liked rooting for him to win. I bawled alongside Jem when he was so shocked his father lost the case. But what does that say about me? To have fallen so hard for Jem's experience when Tom was the one found guilty?

Once again, we see how closely tied Katherine's (1) understanding of race concepts, (2) analysis of literature, and (3) reflection on her own racial identity are in this writing. We argue that the identity work started with learning about foundational race concepts.

Analysis of Race-Based Incidents. Given that race-related incidents happen all the time, we urge students to take the time to analyze race-based incidents in schools. Katherine reflected on an example from her experiences as a student in her high school.

We had race issues going on in our town, most notably the man who lived next to the high school who had a large confederate flag on the back of his property, so it was most prominent when athletes were walking to our athletic fields. It made a lot of other towns very uncomfortable as well as many people in our school. To people of color, that flag is a symbol of hatred, a symbol of oppression by Whites. But a lot of people in our school did not seem to mind it being there and would argue that the man had the right to display it on his property—it's his freedom of speech. And at the end of senior year a bunch of kids from my grade took a group picture in front of it. All of those students were white. None of those students felt personally impacted by the flag as being a symbol of hatred because they were all White students. I realized they weren't just arguing for the man's freedom of speech, as I was excusing it for, but they saw the flag as a symbol of [town] pride. But this only shows that they had the privilege to ignore the other implications for displaying that flag. They could ignore the hatred it meant to people of color because they are white. We could dismiss the issue as a school and as a community because we are predominantly White and the White opinion is the one that holds power in our society. So I can imagine how difficult it would be for my teachers to take on issues of racism in my town.

We see so much race work being done in Katherine's paper as she strives to utilize her emerging racial literacy, particularly through key race concepts like the explanation of White supremacy (although she does not name it in this excerpt), and to apply it to a range of experiences she sees through new eyes. Even though Katherine does not see her work on race and her own racial identity as "done," the effects of having to think about race in these specific ways led to realizations with a lasting impact on her.

Given the importance of feedback to help push students' thinking, the essay is completed in a series of drafts, giving students ample time to reflect on and revise their thinking over the course of half a semester as we continue to read, talk, and analyze texts and world events from a critical race perspective. When we have asked students in interviews or made informal requests for feedback on which facets of our course have had the biggest impact on their racial literacy, even if they reference other assignments, everyone mentions this exploratory essay as seminal in the process.

RACIAL IDENTITY WORK FOR WHITE TEACHERS

There is a threshold of racial literacy that we, as English teachers, need in order to embark on antiracist teaching with our students, because a surface-level understanding not only will not suffice but may end up reinforcing problematic thinking. As we have suggested, the effort to build deep understanding of race-related concepts often leads White teachers and students to "re-see" our own Whiteness, to understand our own White racial identity in new and deeper ways. And in the case of English teachers, understanding of race-related concepts may contribute to "re-seeing" possibilities for antiracist teaching in English curriculum and instruction.

That said, we also know that many White English teachers are unlikely to have encountered in-depth racial literacy instruction, especially around Whiteness, in either K–12 education or teacher education programs. While we call for increased institutional support for this work, many English teachers are left to take it upon themselves if they intend to move racial literacy learning beyond the typical surface-level understanding. What can English teachers do to engage in ways that have an impact on thinking and teaching? Here we have organized recommendations for independent and ongoing racial literacy learning by compiling some of the resources that have been immensely helpful for our own growth.

Deeply Engage with Racial Literacy Resources

Fiction and Nonfiction. Reading literature and other books by and about people of color has been transformative in our personal and professional lives. Some of our favorites include:

- *Americanah* by Chimamanda Adichie
- *Assata: An Autobiography* by Assata Shakur
- *Between the World and Me* by Ta-Nehisi Coates

- *The Book of Night Women* by Marlon James
- *Citizen: An American Lyric* by Claudia Rankine
- *Faces at the Bottom of the Well: The Permanence of Racism* by Derrick Bell
- *The Fire Next Time* by James Baldwin
- *Learning to Be White* by Thandeka
- *Playing in the Dark* and *The Origin of Others* by Toni Morrison
- *Racism Without Racists: Color-blind Racism and the Persistence of Racial Inequality* by Eduardo Bonilla-Silva
- *The Warmth of Other Suns: The Epic Story of America's Great Migration* by Isabel Wilkerson

Of course, this list is limited and partial, but it represents texts that have been powerful in our own learning.

Podcasts, Documentaries, and Films. We have found multimodal resources helpful for filling in some of the gaps in our own racial literacy:

- *Codeswitch*. An NPR radio show hosted by journalists of color, *Codeswitch* explores current events and popular culture, sociological issues, historical events, literature and the arts, and anything else that evokes race and racism in America.
- *Serial: Season Three*. This NPR podcast explores the ins and outs of the Cleveland, Ohio court system. Although journalists did not approach the story from a critical race perspective per se, race and racism emerge as the journalists follow particular judges, cases, and defendants through the legal system.
- *Our National Conversation About Conversations About Race*. The podcast's website says, "Discusses the ways we can't talk, don't talk, would rather not talk, but intermittently, fitfully, embarrassingly do talk about culture, identity, politics, power, and privilege in our pre-post-yet-still-very-racial America. This show is 'About Race.'"
- *The Problem We All Live With, Parts I & II*. In these two episodes of the popular *This American Life* podcast, *New York Times* reporter Nikole Hannah-Jones tells the story of a school district considering integration in Normandy, Missouri, in recent years.
- *Get Out*. Peele's film features Whiteness and its horrors in unsettling and provocative ways. We recommend analyzing the representation of Whiteness in this film as an exercise for building racial literacy.
- *I Am Not Your Negro*. Baldwin's comment, spoken on national television, that became the title for this documentary, focuses on the fact that the "Negro" that has been made in America speaks to

what White Americans think—or need to think—of ourselves; it does not give any information about Black people.

Antiracist Teaching Resources. We also have found these teaching resources valuable:

- *Reading While White.* This blog, created and edited by White librarians, is an excellent example of and resource for White people doing their own work to interrupt racism in the field of children's and young adult literature.
- *Teaching While White.* This collection of resources includes a blog, a podcast, and workshop opportunities designed to explore how Whiteness matters in teaching.
- *Facing History and Ourselves.* This website offers teaching resources organized around topics such as racism in U.S. history, justice and human rights, and global immigration, including unit and lesson plans and multimedia materials that are searchable by discipline.
- *Teaching Tolerance.* This organization supports educators in teaching against hate and oppression of all sorts. It offers free classroom resources, including a subscription to its magazine, lesson plans, film kits, printable posters, and more. It also offers webinars, facilitator guides, and opportunities for self-guided learning.

Develop Critical Partnerships

Engaging in this process of ongoing learning has been bolstered and deepened by our partnership with each other, as well as with colleagues who share similar goals. For each other, we have provided support and accountability. We have read books and articles together, debriefed about issues related to parenting our multiracial children as they have come up, planned for teaching for racial literacy in our courses, and reflected on our practices when things have gone well or not so well. If at all possible, we recommend finding one or a few like-minded colleagues with whom you can collaborate in this endeavor over time. Set up a time to talk, select a common list of books to read or podcasts to listen to. Set goals and develop ideas for taking new steps in your classroom and reflect on those experiences together. If finding such partnerships is difficult where you teach, we have found success in connecting with others through social media and professional conferences.

A BEGINNING, NOT AN END

We see the closing of this book—and the book as a whole—as a beginning for us and, perhaps, for you. It is the work we felt *compelled* to do for years to honor our desires to take action around racial justice through our teaching. Here we offer the best—and still likely limited and partial—ideas we have and have tried out so far to help teachers make deep changes to the ways we prepare White students to understand the role of Whiteness in perpetuating racism.

We see this book as a living document reflecting the current racist waters and our efforts to affect these waters the best way we know how to today, especially in White-dominant English classrooms. But we know that, even if teachers take up some of these practices, students, teachers, institutions, and communities seeking to maintain Whiteness will shift practices in response, requiring teachers to continue to change the ways that we work toward antiracist goals. For this reason, it will be important to test out these practices and to adjust them as you must in order to pursue antiracist work effectively. We hope we get to hear about your efforts to do so. So much depends on all of our efforts to take this on, for the good of us all.

References

Adiche, C. (2009). *The danger of a single story* [YouTube video]. Retrieved from www.ted.com/talks/chimamanda_adichie_the_danger_of_a_single_story?%20 language=en

Allyn, P., & Morrell, E. (2016). *Every child a super reader: 7 strengths to open a world of possible*. New York, NY: Scholastic.

Amobi, F. A. (2007). The message or the messenger: Reflection on the volatility of evoking novice teachers' courageous conversations on race. *Multicultural Education, 14*(3), 2–7.

Anagnostopoulos, D. (2010). *Teaching* To kill a mockingbird *in 21st century American classrooms: Sparking and sustaining discussions of race and racism in the English classroom*. Unpublished manuscript, Department of Teacher Education and Education Policy, Michigan State University, East Lansing.

Applebee, A. N. (1993). *Literature in the secondary schools: Studies in curriculum and instruction in the United States*. Urbana, IL: National Council of Teachers of English.

Appleman, D. (2015). *Critical encounters in secondary English: Teaching literary theory to adolescents* (3rd ed.). New York, NY: Teachers College Press.

Arac, J. (2004). Huckleberry Finn as idol and target. In G. Graff & J. Phelan (Eds.), *Adventures of Huckleberry Finn: A case study in critical controversy* (2nd ed., pp. 435–456). Boston, MA: Bedford/St. Martin's. (Original work published 1997)

Asher, N. (2007). Made in the (multicultural) U.S.A.: Unpacking the tensions of race, culture, gender, and sexuality in education. *Educational Researcher, 36*(2), 65–73.

Baker-Bell, A. (2017). "I can switch my language, but I can't switch my skin": What teachers must understand about linguistic racism. In E. Moore & A. Michael (Eds.), *The guide for white women who teach black boys* (pp. 97–107). Thousand Oaks, CA: Corwin Press.

Baker-Bell, A., Butler, T., & Johnson, L. (2017). The pain and the wounds: A call for critical race English education in the wake of racial violence. *English Education, 49*(2), 116-129.

Baldwin, J. (1963). *The fire next time*. New York, NY: Dial.

Banks, J. A. (2001). Approaches to multicultural curriculum reform. In J. A. Banks

& C. A. McGee Banks (Eds.), *Multicultural education: Issues and perspectives* (4th ed., pp. 225–246). Hoboken, NJ: Wiley.

Beach, R. (1993). *A teacher's introduction to reader-response theories.* Urbana, IL: National Council of Teachers of English.

Beach, R., Thein, A. H., & Parks, D. (2008). *High school students' competing social worlds.* Mahwah, NJ: Erlbaum.

Bell, D. (1992). *Faces at the bottom of the well: The permanence of racism.* New York, NY: HarperCollins.

Berchini, C. (2016). Structuring contexts: Pathways toward un-obstructing race-consciousness. *International Journal of Qualitative Studies in Education, 29*(8), 1030–1044.

Berchini, C. (2019). Reconceptualizing whiteness in English education: Failure, fraughtness, and accounting for context. *English Education, 51*(2), 151–181.

Bishop, R. S. (1990). Mirrors, windows, and sliding glass doors. *Perspectives, 6*(3), ix–xi.

Bolgatz, J. (2005). *Talking race in the classroom.* New York, NY: Teachers College Press.

Bonilla-Silva, E. (2013). *Racism without racists: Color-blind racism and the persistence of racial inequality* (4th ed.). Lanham, MD: Rowman & Littlefield.

Borsheim-Black, C. (2012). *"Not as multicultural as I'd like": White English teachers' uses of literature for multicultural education in predominantly white contexts.* Unpublished manuscript, Department of Curriculum, Instruction, and Teacher Education, Michigan State University, East Lansing.

Borsheim-Black, C. (2015). "It's pretty much white": Challenges and opportunities of an anti-racist approach to literature instruction in a multi-layered white context. *Research in the Teaching of English, 49*(4), 407–429.

Borsheim-Black, C. (2018). "You could argue it either way": Ambivalent white teacher racial identity and teaching about racism in literature study. *English Education, 50*(3), 228–254.

Borsheim-Black, C., Macaluso, M., & Petrone, R. (2014). Critical literature pedagogy: Teaching canonical literature for critical pedagogy. *Journal of Adolescent & Adult Literacy, 58*(2), 123–133.

Boyd, F. B. (2002). Conditions, concessions, and the many tender mercies of learning through multicultural literature. *Literacy Research and Instruction, 42*(1), 58–92.

Burke, J. (2010). *What's the big idea? Question-driven units to motivate reading, writing, and thinking.* Portsmouth, NH: Heinemann.

Butler, T. T. (2017). # Say[ing]HerName as critical demand: English education in the age of erasure. *English Education, 49*(2), 153–178.

Chadwick-Joshua, J. (1998). *The Jim dilemma: Reading race in* Huckleberry Finn. Jackson: University Press of Mississippi.

Chenelle, S., & Fisch, A. (2014). Using informational text to teach *To kill a mockingbird.* Lanham, MD: Rowman & Littlefield Education.

Chestnutt, C. W. (2001). The passing of Grandison. In S. H. Ferguson (Ed.), *Charles W. Chestnutt: Selected writings*. New York, NY: Houghton Mifflin. (Original work published 1898)

Christensen, L. (2015). Rethinking research: Reading and writing about the roots of gentrification. *English Journal, 105*(2), 15–21.

Coates, T. N. (2015). *Between the world and me*. New York, NY: Spiegel & Grau.

Collins, S. (2008). *The hunger games*. Hoboken, NJ: Wiley & Sons.

Cooperative Children's Book Center. (2016). Publishing statistics on children's books about people of color and first/native nations and by people of color and first/native nations authors and illustrators. School of Education, University of Wisconsin–Madison. Retrieved from ccbc.education.wisc.edu/books/pcstats.asp

Delgado, R. (1989). Storytelling for oppositionists and others: A plea for narrative. *Michigan Law Review, 87*(8), 2411–2441.

Delgado, R., & Stefancic, J. (2001). *Critical race theory: An introduction*. New York, NY: NYU Press.

DiAngelo, R. (2016). *What does it mean to be white? Developing white racial literacy* (rev. ed.). New York: Peter Lang.

DiAngelo, R. (2018, October 1). Why "I'm not racist" is only half the story [YouTube video]. Retrieved from www.youtube.com/watch?v=kzLT54QjclA

Dressel, J. H. (2005). Personal response and social responsibility: Responses of middle school students to multicultural literature. *The Reading Teacher, 58*(8), 750–764.

Dyches, J. (2018). Critical canon pedagogy: Applying disciplinary inquiry to cultivate canonical critical consciousness. *Harvard Educational Review, 88*(4), 538–564.

Fisher, R. & Petryk, T. (2017). *Balancing asymmetrical social power dynamics* (Working Paper No. 3). University of Michigan Program on Intergroup Relations.

Fox, D. L., & Short, K. G. (2003). *Stories matter: The complexity of cultural authenticity in children's literature*. Urbana, IL: National Council of Teachers of English.

Frankenberg, R. (1993). *White women, race matters: The social construction of whiteness*. Minneapolis: University of Minnesota Press.

Freire, P. (1970). *Pedagogy of the oppressed*. New York, NY: Continuum.

Garcia, A., & Haddix, M. (2014). The revolution starts with Rue. In S. P. Connors (Ed.), *The politics of panem: Challenging genres* (pp. 203–217). Rotterdam: Netherlands, Sense Publishers.

Glazier, J. (2003). Moving closer to speaking the unspeakable: White teachers talking about race. *Teacher Education Quarterly, 30*(2), 73–94.

Glazier, J., & Seo, J. A. (2005). Multicultural literature and discussion as mirror and window? *Journal of Adolescent & Adult Literacy, 48*(8), 686–700.

Glenn, W. J. (2014). To witness and to testify: Preservice teachers examine literary aesthetics to better understand diverse literature. *English Education, 46*(2), 90–116.

Gordon, J. (2005). Inadvertent complicity: Colorblindness in teacher education. *Education Studies, 38*(2), 135–153.

Greenfield, L. (2011). The "standard English" fairy tale: A rhetorical analysis of racist pedagogies and commonplace assumptions about language diversity. In L. Greenfield & K. Rowan (Eds.), *Writing centers and the new racism: A call for sustainable dialogue and change* (pp. 18–60). Logan: Utah State University Press.

Grinage, J. (2013). Combating Huck Finn's censorship: A step-by-step guide to discussing the n-word in the classroom. In S. Grineski, J. Landsman, & R. Simmons, III (Eds.), *Talking about race: Alleviating the fear* (pp. 137–148). Sterling, VA: Stylus.

Groenke, S. L., Haddix, M., Glenn, W. J., Kirkland, D. E., Price-Dennis, D., & Coleman-King, C. (2015). Disrupting and dismantling the dominant vision of youth of color. *English Journal, 104*(3), 35–40.

Guinier, L. (2004). From racial liberalism to racial literacy: *Brown v. Board of Education* and the interest-divergence dilemma. *The Journal of American History, 91*(1), 92–118.

Haddix, M., & Price-Dennis, D. (2013). Urban fiction and multicultural literature as transformative tools for preparing English teachers for diverse classrooms. *English Education, 45*(3), 247–283.

Hamilton, S. (2016) *Essential literary terms: A brief Norton guide with exercises,* (2nd ed.). New York, NY: W.W. Norton & Company.

Hannah-Jones, N. (Reporter). (2015, July 31). The problem we all live with [Audio podcast]. *This American Life.* Retrieved from www.thisamericanlife.org/562/the-problem-we-all-live-with-part-one/act-one-0

Haviland, V. (2008). "Things get glossed over": Rearticulating the silencing power of whiteness in education. *Journal of Teacher Education, 59*(1), 40–54.

Helms, J. E. (1990). *Black and white racial identity: Theory, research, and practice.* Westport, CT: Greenwood Press.

Henderson, L. (2005). The black arts movement and African American young adult literature: An evaluation of narrative style. *Children's Literature in Education, 36*(4), 299–323.

Henry, P. (2004). The struggle for tolerance: Race and censorship in *Huckleberry Finn*. In G. Graff & J. Phelan (Eds.), *Adventures of Huckleberry Finn: A case study in critical controversy* (2nd ed., pp. 382–405). Boston, MA: Bedford/St. Martin's. (Original work published 1992)

Holden-Smith, B. (1996). Lynching, federalism, and the intersection of race and gender in the progressive era. *Yale Journal of Law & Feminism, 8*, 31\–78.

Horner, M. (2019). Resistance, reception, race, and rurality: Teaching non-canonical texts in a white, conservative Montana context. In M. V. Blackburn (Ed.), *Adventurous thinking: Students' rights to read and write.* Urbana, IL: National Council of Teachers of English.

Huber, L. P., Johnson, R. N., & Kohli, R. (2006). Naming racism: A conceptual look at internalized racism in U.S. schools. *Chicana/o Latina/o Law Review, 26*, 183–206.

Janks, H. (2002) Critical literacy: Beyond reason. *Australian Educational Researcher, 29*, 7–27.

Jemisin, N.K. (2019). *How long 'til black future month?* London, England: Orbit Books.

Johnson, E. (2013). Embodying English: Performing and positioning the white teacher in a high school English class. *English Education, 46*(1), 5–33.

Johnson, L. L. (2018). Where do we go from here? Toward a critical race English education. *Research in the Teaching of English, 53*(2), 102–124.

Johnson, L. L., Jackson, J., Stovall, D. O., & Baszile, D. T. (2017). "Loving blackness to death": (Re)Imagining ELA classrooms in a time of racial chaos. *English Journal, 106*(4), 60–66.

Kailin, J. (2002). *Antiracist education: From theory to practice.* Lanham, MD: Rowman & Littlefield.

Kaplan, R.G. & Garcia, A. (2019). Afrofuturist reading: Exploring non-western depictions of magical worlds in Akata Witch. In R. Ginsberg & W.J. Glenn (Eds.), *Engaging with multicultural YA literature in the secondary classroom: Critical approaches for critical educators* (pp. 180–190). New York, NY: Routledge.

Kennedy, R. (2008). *Nigger: The strange career of a troublesome word.* New York, NY: Vintage Books.

Kirkland, D. (2013). *A search past silence: The literacy of young black men.* New York, NY: Teachers College Press.

Kolbas, E. D. (2018). *Critical theory and the literary canon.* New York, NY: Routledge.

Ladson-Billings, G., & Tate, W. F. (1995). Toward a critical race theory of education. *Teachers College Record, 97*(1), 47–68.

Lee, H. (1982). *To kill a mockingbird.* New York, NY: Warner Books. (Original work published in 1960)

Leer, E. (2010). *Multicultural literature in monocultural classrooms: White teachers explore diverse texts with white students.* Lewiston, NY: Edwin Mellen Press.

Lensmire, T., McManimon, S., Tierney, J. D., Lee-Nichols, M., Casey, Z., Lensmire, A., & Davis, B. (2013). McIntosh as synecdoche: How teacher education's focus on white privilege undermines antiracism. *Harvard Educational Review, 83*(3), 410–431.

Leonardo, Z. (2004). The color of supremacy: Beyond the discourse of "white privilege." *Educational Philosophy and Theory, 36*(2), 137–152.

Lester, J. (2004). Morality and *Adventures of Huckleberry Finn.* In G. Graff & J. Phelan (Eds.), *Adventures of Huckleberry Finn: A case study in critical controversy* (2nd ed., pp. 362–370). Boston, MA: Bedford/St. Martin's. (Original work published 1984)

Lewis, C. (2000). Critical issues: Limits of identification: The personal, pleasurable, and critical in reader response. *Journal of Literacy Research, 32*(2), 253–266.

Lewis, C., Ketter, J., & Fabos, B. (2001). Reading race in a rural context. *Qualitative Studies in Education, 14*(3), 317–350.

Lipsitz, G. (2006). *The possessive investment in whiteness: How white people profit from identity politics.* Philadelphia, PA: Temple University Press.

Lipsky, S. (1987). *Internalized racism.* Seattle, WA: Rational Island.

Love, B. L. (2017). Difficult knowledge: When a black feminist educator was too afraid to #SayHerName. *English Education, 49,* 192–208.

Lowenstein, K. L. (2009). The work of multicultural teacher education: Reconceptualizing white teacher candidates as learners. *Review of Educational Research, 79*(1), 163–196.

Macaluso, M. (2017). Teaching *To kill a mockingbird* today: Coming to terms with race, racism, and America's novel. *Journal of Adolescent & Adult Literacy, 61*(3), 279–287.

Macaluso, M. and Macaluso, K. (Eds.). (2018). *Teaching the canon in 21st century classrooms.* Leiden: Brill/Sense.

Marx, S., & Pennington, J. (2003). Pedagogies of critical race theory: Experimentations with white preservice teachers. *International Journal of Qualitative Studies in Education, 16*(1), 91–110.

Matias, C. E. (2016). *Feeling white: Whiteness, emotionality, and education.* New York, NY: Springer.

McCormick, K. (1994). *The culture of reading and the teaching of English.* Manchester, UK: Manchester University Press.

McIntosh, P. (1989). White privilege: Unpacking the invisible knapsack. *Race, Class, and Gender in the United States, 6,* 188–192.

McIntyre, A. (1997). *Making meaning of whiteness: Exploring racial identity with white teachers.* Albany: State University of New York Press.

Mitchell, K. (2019). The N-word in the classroom: Just say NO [Audio podcast]. Retrieved from soundcloud.com/c19podcast/nword

Moll, L. C., Amanti, C., Neff, D., & Gonzalez, N. (1992). Funds of knowledge for teaching: Using a qualitative approach to connect homes and classrooms. *Theory into Practice, 31*(2), 132–141.

Morrell, E. (2005). Critical English education. *English Education, 37*(4), 312–321.

Morrell, E. (2015). *Critical literacy and urban youth: Pedagogies of access, dissent, and liberation.* New York, NY: Routledge.

Morrell, E. (2018, May). *Teaching and race in the literacy classroom.* Paper presented at the Building Cultural Literacy Webinar series, Waterford Township, MI.

Morrison, T. (1992). *Playing in the dark: Whiteness and the literary imagination.* Cambridge, MA: Harvard University Press.

Morrison, T. (2017). *The origin of others.* Cambridge, MA: Harvard University Press.

Mullins, M. (2016). Counter-counterstorytelling: Rereading critical race theory in Percival Everett's *Assumption. Callaloo, 39*(2), 457–472.

National Council of Teachers of English. (2015a). *Resolution on the need for diverse children's and young adult books.* Urbana, IL: Author. Retrieved from www2.ncte.org/statement/diverse-books/

National Council of Teachers of English. (2015b). Statement affirming

#BlackLivesMatter. Urbana, IL: Author. Retrieved from www.ncte.org/gover-nance/pres-team_9-8-15

NCTE. (2012). *NCTE program standards: Program for the initial preparation of teachers in secondary English language arts.* Urbana, IL: National Council of Teachers of English.

Obear, K. (2017). *Training the facilitators: Deepening capacity to lead equity and inclusion sessions.* Center for Transformation and Change. Retrieved from drkathyobear.com

Paris, D., & Alim, H. S. (Eds.). (2017). *Culturally sustaining pedagogies: Teaching and learning for justice in a changing world.* New York, NY: Teachers College Press.

Pasque, P. A., Chesler, M. A., Charbeneau, J., & Carlson, C. (2013). Pedagogical approaches to student racial conflict in the classroom. *Journal of Diversity in Higher Education, 6*(1), 1–16.

Petrone, R. (2015). *Learning as loss: Examining student resistance and the affective dimensions to learning critical literacy.* National Council of Teachers of English Annual Conference, Minneapolis, MN.

Pollock, M. (2004). *Colormute: Race talk dilemmas in an American school.* Princeton, NJ: Princeton University Press.

Rabinowitz, P., & Smith, M. W. (1997). *Authorizing readers: Resistance and respect in the teaching of literature.* New York, NY: Teachers College Press.

Ramage, J. D., Bean, J. C., & Johnson, J. (2009). Writing an exploratory essay or annotated bibliography. In *The Allyn & Bacon guide to writing, brief edition* (5th ed., pp. 175–207). New York, NY: Pearson.

Reyes, A. (2011) "Racist!": Metapragmatic regimentation of racist discourse by Asian American youth. *Discourse & Society, 22*(4), 458–473.

Rogers, R., & Mosley, M. (2006). Racial literacy in a second grade classroom: Critical race theory, whiteness studies, and literacy research. *Reading Research Quarterly, 41*(4), 462–495.

Rosenblatt, L. (1995). *Literature as exploration* (5th ed.). New York, NY: Modern Language Association of America.

Sassi, K., & Thomas, E. E. (2008). Walking the talk: Examining privilege and race in a ninth-grade classroom. *English Journal,* pp. 25–31.

Savini, C. (2011). *ENGL 105: English Composition* [Course syllabus]. Westfield, MA: English Department, Westfield State University.

Scheurich, J. J., & Young, M. (1997). Coloring epistemologies: Are our research epistemologies racially biased? *American Educational Research Journal, 26*(4), 4–16.

Sealey-Ruiz, Y., & Greene, P. (2015). Popular visual images and the (mis) reading of black male youth: A case for racial literacy in urban preservice teacher education. *Teaching Education, 26*(1), 55–76.

Sigward, D. (2014). *Teaching mockingbird.* Facing History and Ourselves National Foundation. Retrieved from www.facinghistory.org/mockingbird

Singleton, G. E. (2006). *Courageous conversations about race: A field guide for achieving equity in schools.* Thousand Oaks, CA: Corwin Press.

Skerrett, A. (2011). English teachers' racial literacy knowledge and practice. *Race, Ethnicity and Education, 14*(3), 313–330.

Sleeter, C. E. (2011). Reflections on my use of multicultural and critical pedagogy when students are white. In K. L. Koppelman (Ed.), *Perspectives on human differences* (pp. 315–319). Boston, MA: Pearson.

Smagorinsky, P. (2007). *Teaching English by design: How to create and carry out instructional units.* Portsmouth, NH: Heinemann.

Smiley, J. (2004). Say it ain't so, Huck: Second thoughts on Mark Twain's "masterpiece." In G. Graff & J. Phelan (Eds.), *Adventures of Huckleberry Finn: A case study in critical controversy* (2nd ed., pp. 456–466). Boston, MA: Bedford/St. Martin's. (Original work published 1996)

Smitherman, G. (1999). *Talkin that talk: Language, culture and education in African America.* New York, NY: Routledge.

SparkNotes Editors. (2002). SparkNote on *to kill a mockingbird.* Retrieved from www.sparknotes.com/lit/mocking/

Spring, J. (2016). *Deculturalization and the struggle for equality: A brief history of the education of dominated cultures in the United States.* New York, NY: Routledge.

Stallworth, B. J., Gibbons, L., & Fauber, L. (2006). It's not on the list: An exploration of teachers' perspectives on using multicultural literature. *Journal of Adolescent & Adult Literacy, 49*(6), 478–489.

Sue, D. W. (2015). *Race talk and the conspiracy of silence: Understanding and facilitating difficult dialogues on race.* Hoboken, NJ: Wiley.

Tanner, S. J. (2019). Whiteness is a white problem: Whiteness in English Education. *English Education, 51*(2), 182–199.

Tatum, B. D. (2000). *Why are all the Black kids sitting together in the cafeteria? And other conversations about race.* New York, NY: Basic Books.

Thandeka. (1999). *Learning to be white: Money, race and god in America.* New York, NY: Continuum.

Thein, A. H. (November, 2011). *Avoiding the pitfalls of political correctness, politeness, and persuasion: An authentic approach to perspective-taking in discussions of multicultural literature.* National Council of Teachers of English, Chicago, IL.

Thomas, E. E. (2015). "We always talk about race": Navigating race talk dilemmas in the teaching of literature. *Research in the Teaching of English, 50*(2), 154–175.

Thomas, E. E. (2018). Q & A with Ebony Elizabeth Thomas: Why children need more diverse books. PennGSE Newsroom. Retrieved from www.gse.upenn.edu/news/ebony-elizabeth-thomas-diverse-books-children

Thomas, E. E. (2019). *The dark fantastic: Race and the imagination from Harry Potter to the Hunger Games.* New York, NY: NYU Press.

Thompson, A. (2003). Tiffany, friend of people of color: White investments in antiracism. *International Journal of Qualitative Studies in Education, 16*(1), 7–29.

Toliver, S. R. (2018). Alterity and innocence: *The hunger games*, Rue, and black girl adultification. *Journal of Children's Literature, 44*(2), 4–15.

Trainor, J. S. (2005). "My ancestors didn't own slaves": Understanding white talk about race. *Research in the Teaching of English, 40*(2), 140–167.

Traver, R. (1998, March). What is a good guiding question? *Educational Leadership, 55*(6), 70–73.

Twain, M. (with O'Meally, R. G.). (2003). *The adventures of Huckleberry Finn.* New York, NY: Barnes & Noble. (Original work published 1884).

Twine, F. W. (2004). A white side of black Britain: The concept of racial literacy. *Ethnic and Racial Studies, 27*(6), 878–907.

Underwood, W. (1987). The body biography: A framework for student writing. *English Journal, 76*(8), 44–48.

Wiggins, G., & McTighe, J. (2005). *Understanding by design* (2nd ed.). Alexandria, VA: Association for Supervision and Curriculum Development.

Wilhelm, J. (2007). *Engaging readers and writers with inquiry: Promoting deep understandings in the language arts and content areas through guiding questions.* New York, NY: Scholastic.

Williams, L. (2008). *From Flint, Michigan to your front door: Tracing the roots of racism.* RaceBridges Studio. Retrieved from racebridgesstudio.com/from-flint-michigan-to-your-front-door-tracing-the-roots-of-racism-in-america/

Wolfe, B. (1949). Uncle Remus and the malevolent rabbit: Readings in the interpretation of Afro-American folklore. In A. Dundas (Ed.), *Mother wit from laughing barrel* (pp. 524–540). Jackson: University of Mississippi Press.

Index

About the Authors

Carlin Borsheim-Black is associate professor of English education at Central Michigan University where she teaches young adult literature and literature methods courses. Her scholarship and teaching focus on critical approaches to literature instruction, especially the challenges and possibilities of anti-racist literature instruction in rural and predominantly White spaces.

Sophia Tatiana Sarigianides is professor of English education at Westfield State University where she teaches young adult literature and methods courses. Her scholarship and teaching focus on interrogating adolescence in young adult literature and in teacher and youth thinking, and the study of race and racism in texts.